P9-DHS-874

WITHDRAWN

EX LIBRIS

SOUTH ORANGE
PUBLIC LIBRARY

WITHDRAWN

A
CENTURY
OF BAGS

A CENTURY OF BAGS

ICONS OF STYLE IN THE 20TH CENTURY
CLAIRE WILCOX

CHARTWELL
BOOKS, INC.

OS
391.4
Wil

A QUARTO BOOK

Published by Chartwell Books
A Division of Book Sales, Inc.
114, Northfield Avenue
Edison, New Jersey 08837

This edition produced for sale in the U.S.A.,
its territories and dependencies only.

Copyright © 1997 Quarto Inc.
All rights reserved.
No part of this publication may be reproduced,
stored in a retrieval system or transmitted in any
form or by any means, electronic, mechanical,
photocopying, recording or otherwise, without
the permission of the copyright holder.

ISBN 0-7858-0834-5

This book was designed and produced by
Quarto Publishing plc
6 Blundell Street
London N7 9BH

Project Editors Tom Whyte, Marilyn Inglis
Editors Henrietta Wilkinson, Maggi McCormick,
Jennifer Baines, Rebecca Moy
Editorial Director Gilly Cameron Cooper

Designer Paul Hetherington
Design Assistants Sabine Heitz,
David Kemp
Assistant Art Director Penny Cobb
Picture Researcher Miriam Hyman
Photographer Richard Gleed
Art Director Moira Clinch

Manufactured in Singapore by Eray Scan Pte Ltd
Printed in China by Leefung-Asco Printers Ltd

Contents

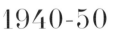
Zabel 8/19/98 25:58

Introduction

1950s evening bag (*above*) by Lujean of Madison Avenue, New York, made of machine-made, black lace over "nude" satin, gathered onto a metal frame set with simulated pearls.

Beautifully made reticule in leather inlaid with tortoiseshell and mother-of-pearl, reminiscent of marquetry work in furniture, Germany, 1820.

Throughout this century, the handbag has faithfully mirrored women's occupations and aspirations. On the one hand, bags are entirely practical and on the other, they are the stuff of fantasy, their interiors capable of guarding our dreams and secrets. Psychoanalysts have long been aware of their symbolic significance, while cartoonists and satirical writers, from Punch magazine to Oscar Wilde, have repeatedly lampooned the unfortunate bag in its many forms.

Over the decades, the bag has been the subject of intense consumer desire, and its more successful designs have achieved cult status and have been identified with leading female figures such as Grace Kelly, Jacqueline Onassis, Margaret Thatcher, and Queen Elizabeth II. The changes in its shape and purpose have charted the rise of the professional woman, among many other social developments, while its design and decoration have reflected all manner of artistic movements from Art Nouveau through Surrealism to Pop Art.

From Pocket to Purse

Early in the 1800s, the first bags developed in response to changing fashions in dress. With the slender, neo-classical styles of around 1800, garments became too flimsy and close fitting to conceal pockets, which were then separate garments usually made of plain washable cotton. They were attached to tapes which were tied around the waist, and were reached through slashes in the side of the skirt. Pockets were later made as part of the lining of the skirt, but by then the vogue for handbags had become established. They went on to become an essential accessory for many women.

At first, handbags were used to transport the ephemera connected with womens' social lives, from dance cards to diaries, fans, pocket handkerchiefs, letters, and visiting cards. Such bags became known as "indispensables" in Britain and "ridicules" in France, and were naturally the subject of gentle humor, as befitted an item that had made the transition from private to public life. As the 19th century progressed, the term "ridicule" evolved into "reticule", a term that was used in both French and English up to 1912.

Early fabric reticules were either gently gathered with silk cord or were shaped and flat. The flat reticule resembed the humble pocket, and was often stiffened with card, many made at home as demonstrations of a young lady's skill with her hands. Fabric bags provided every opportunity for decoration in

the form of embroidery, beadwork, and lace, some made as gifts, others part of a coordinated outfit of dress and bag. Today's bag collectors particularly prize those which are dated.

Such bags reflected the changing fashions in printed and woven textiles and embroidery. Silk cross stitch on a canvas base was hugely popular in the 1830s and 1840s, soon followed by a craze for Berlin woolwork in the 1850s and 1860s. Before long, handbags were not just made from fabric, but fashioned out of metal, raffia, leather, ivory — anything that could be shaped to contain small personal items.

Many reticules and early purses from the 1800s still survive, some beautifully made at home, others stitched by professionals. Among the most collectible items are exquisitely beaded or embroidered bags, and especially those in good condition. Older embroidered bags have often faded with time, and while glass beads fortunately do not lose their color as embroidery does, the threads that hold them can be very fragile. Gleaming, faceted beads of cut steel were often used to decorate late Victorian bags and miser's purses—a long shape with enclosing rings which slide down to open—but these have often rusted if they have been stored in a damp environment.

Metal coin purses on long chains which were worn around the neck are highly sought after too, as are rigid, hinged purses made from fragile shell, ivory, and tortoiseshell, with their silk-lined interiors. A bag in good condition inside will always fetch more than one that is not, and leather or fabric frame bags from later on in the century often have pristine interiors, protected over the years from light and dirt.

The Handbag as a Fashion Accessory

Handbags soon became decorative satellites of the dominant moods of fashion, reflecting first the languid, early 1800s look, then the full skirted look, and the tailored dress silhouette as the century progressed. Crinoline skirts became fashionable in the 1860s, accompanied by chatelaine bags and purses worn at the waist to carry keys, scissors, and money. These styles were part of a nostalgic revival of the medieval idea of the mistress of the house, albeit influenced by notions of a woman's role as housekeeper.

Chatelaines did have a functional purpose – they left the hands free to

A papier mâché bag (*left*) in a neo-classical shape, in the form of a Grecian urn, 1800s . A printed, velvet evening bag (*right*) of 1966, made in Italy by Emilio Pucci, is typical of his abstract, pattern designs

Small, dainty, beaded purse (*below*) with metal, twist-lock clasp.

Early 1900s, fabric velvet and gold gaming bag (*left*) gathered with drawstring. Stylish, black handbags (*far left*) from the Joan and David Spring Collection, 1996, with narrow straps, horizontal leather trim and interlocking oval clasp.

manage the long skirts of the time or to carry a larger shopping bag, parasol, or muff when outdoors — but many of their miniature accessories, from scissors to perfume bottles, were purely decorative. The most expensive, made from silver and hung from a silver linked belt, were worn both inside the house and when visiting or shopping, right up to the early 1900s.

The term "hand-bag" was used from the mid 1800s onwards, but generally referred to fairly substantial leather bags attached to a metal or wooden frame. These had been developed by leatherworkers in the saddlery trade rather than dressmakers, and were called "hand-bags" in order to distinguish them from other items of travel baggage. Their manufacture and styling were greatly influenced by developments in the dyeing and processing of leather, particularly in Germany, and by the early 1900s, leather bags were available in a multitude of bright colors.

As the leather handbag became more widely used, the term gradually became applicable to more styles of bag. The terms "pocketbook" and "purse" also became widespread in the United States, used to refer to a range of styles all of which were known as "handbags" in Britain, where a purse was, and still is, a container for small change, which the Americans call a "change purse".

The Modern Bag

By the early 1900s, reticules and handbags were well established as a fashionable accessory, considered the perfect finishing touch to any outfit. Leather, lizard, and crocodile were the height of chic, while other bags were made from fabric, or silver mesh, for evening wear. Bags continued to reflect the changes in fashion and taste, becoming more exotic during the rage for Orientalism that swept Europe early in the century, and more restrained after the onset of World War 1.

By the 1920s, handbags had come into their own. Beaded bags patterned in jazzy patterns swung with the beaded dance dresses of the flappers who seemed to epitomize the Roaring Twenties. These modern women with cropped hair dared to smoke and powder their noses in public, and the rise in the use of both cigarettes and cosmetics by women led to a range of attractive, especially designed accessories. Before long, rigid, molded plastics imitating tortoiseshell

Tough, nylon fold-up case (*below*) in bright colours from Longchamp, forming part of the company's modern, new look, 1970s.

Late 1940s, early 1950s advertisement from Simpson of Piccadilly, featuring red leather casual drawstring bag—note the smart gloves and hat, even with such an informal outfit.

Station scene (*above*) showing a collection of flat-topped, leather luggage, ranging in date from 1850 to 1910. White shoulder bags (*right*) with substantial metal ring clasps and chain straps. Salvatore Ferragamo, Italy.

Two rhinestone encrusted evening bags (*right*) in the form of violas, from the inimitable American designer, Judith Leiber, 1990s.

and ivory were being shaped into vanity boxes, lipstick holders, and compacts.

By the 1920s, no stylish woman would be seen without a pochette, which tucked under the arm and perfectly suited the slim, short-skirted silhouette of the day. Their flat, rectangular shape ideally suited the geometric abstract Art Deco patterns that were the flavor of the time, drawing on Egyptian archaeological discoveries and Chinese sources for inspiration.

Economic confidence and stability in Europe and America proved hard to regain, and by the 1930s, the idea of the "good" handbag which would last for decades, thanks to its quality manufacture, was taking hold. Handbags had a modern streamlined quality but became plainer, providing a stable, mature accent to an outfit rather than providing one part of an ensemble of various decorative components, as in the 1920s. Good quality frames and plain materials were enough in themselves, offset with a sparkling, diamanté clasp or stylish, marcasite monogram.

From Practical Back to Decorative

This practical emphasis on handbag design was extended during the war years of the 1940s, when bags became very expensive and beyond the reach of most women (although they were not actually rationed). Narrow skirts, tailored jackets, and shoulder-length hair were seen everywhere in Europe and America during the war, and such utility fashions teamed up with military-influenced designs to promote the shoulder bag, which was perfect for carrying gas masks, ration coupons, and identity cards.

Women's magazines encouraged women to try their hand at making their own handbags from scraps of fabric, and while "make do and mend" challenged women's ingenuity at first, by the end of the war many women longed for a relief from austerity. Nonetheless, rationing continued in Europe through the first years after the war, and metal and leather continued to be in short supply.

It was 1947 before fashion recovered from wartime restrictions, kickstarted by the French designer, Christian Dior. Dior's New Look of 1947 sent the shoulder bag straight to the bottom of the wardrobe, as military associations were the last thing that women wanted—and anyway, it looked quite wrong with the extravagantly full, long skirts, fitted bodices, high heels, and ladylike

Substantial, blue leather handbag (*below*) with white topstitching and brass trimmings, Goldpfeil.

Judith Leiber shell bag (*right*) of 1972—fragile and beautiful, this bag is a collector's item.

Chanel handbags (*above*) featuring plush-bound handles with double-C logo, 1995-6.

hat of the New Look. This required a bag that indicated leisure, femininity, and impracticality, and only the new, slim pochette shape would do.

Bags remained an expensive luxury item until the boom of the 1950s, however, when a choice of handbags filled the shops, from mass-produced, wipe-clean, cheap plastic bags to those made from expensive crocodile. The philosophy of the 1950s was that every woman should invest in a good bag and a matching pair of shoes for daytime wear, and something more glamorous for evening use.

In Step with the Teenager

Towards the end of the 1950s, the cult of the teenager was born. There had been the beginnings of a youth culture in the late 1940s with popular singers such as Frank Sinatra, one of the first teen idols, but society had never seen anything quite like the "baby-boomers" before, as they began to rewrite the rules for everything, and especially fashion.

Within five years, the social revolution was manifesting itself in fashion and design, incorporating modern, space-age pre-occupations and radical developments in the plastics and synthetics industry. Synthetic leathers developed by the automobile industry for car interiors were soon being used by accessory manufacturers, and handbag design underwent its own revolution.

Dynamic bags were made in modern materials such as shiny plastic patents, waterproof PVC (polyvinyl chloride impregnated fabric), vinyl, cast Perspex for handles, linked plastics and metals, printed paper, and synthetic fabrics of all kinds. The youthful vitality of the mini skirt and the liberation of the trouser suit fashions demanded a new handbag style, and young designers were soon setting up their own companies. Before long, small, neat bags swinging on long shoulder chains were a threat to every passer by.

The young flocked to the Indian sub-continent on the "hippy trail" and brought back some of the culture, bringing an ethnic look to clothes and bags. Popular music also had an enormous influence on the fashionable dress of the young, although a mood of nostalgia and romanticism crept into fashion in the late 1970s, epitomized by the British boutique Biba. The country look also came into vogue, and satchels, fishing bags, and sturdy shoulder bags with brass trimmings were seen on the shoulder of countless town dwellers as they became preoccupied with escaping the urban sprawl.

With the high-earning jobs and power dressing of the 80s, efficient black handbags and briefcases with corners sharp enough to graze a passing commuter were commonplace. Handbags managed to achieve cult status and significance in a way that other accessories did not. This was despite the demise of the "one good bag" as an investment, and the arrival of a plethora of new designs and materials. Even so, some styles remained absolute classics, as if their existence was so firmly rooted in women's subconscious that they had become part of a common tradition, and nothing could budge them.

As women's lives opened up and the demands upon their bags changed, rough, everyday use became possible thanks to a range of new materials, from nylon coatings, waterproof leather, sophisticated fastenings, and molded plastics to lightweight fabrics. All have led to a greater flexibility and choice in bags, an essential adjustment in an era when the things that women put in their handbags have changed radically, sometimes even including cellphones and laptop computers.

Functional, fashionable, and frivolous, handbags are part of a woman's fashionable identity. Do they reveal the woman? The exterior may, but the inner contents still remain one of modern women's best-kept secrets. Getting the best out of life may not always be dependent on a good bag, but it certainly helps.

Exquisite, little blue bag (*above*) designed by Paul Smith.

Shiny, bright, structured handbags (*right*) from the cult company Prada, with covered frames, 1997-8.

New Attitudes For a New Era

The dawn of the new century did not herald an immediate change in fashion. Accessories took time to accommodate to altered lifestyles, and many society women remained aloof from the handbag. Having no need to carry money or keys, they preferred to use tiny decorative purses or pouches for their trifles, leaving bags to those of more humble origins. But the handbag soon became a luxurious fashion statement, a symbol of spirited fun and frivolity which acted as an antidote to the grimness of

World War I. By the turn of the 20th century, women were significant wage earners and consumers. In the United States, a fifth of the female population was employed, mostly in the clothing industry and manufacture of fashion accessories, and low labor costs fueled a rising wave of consumerism. Women's magazines overflowed with articles on the latest fashions and ideas on how and what to buy. Even for the less affluent, the clothing and shopping markets in Europe and America were rich with choice, as quantities of imported goods filled department stores and mail-order catalogs such as that produced by the mail order company Sears, Roebuck. Department stores did not simply buy in designs; they commissioned their own for all occasions, including tempting Christmas presents and suitable wedding gifts.

Militant suffragette Mrs Emmeline Pankhurst advocated radical tactics to achieve the vote for women. Her business-like rectangular bag would not look out of place today. A beautifully made turn of the century gold-colored metallic mesh bag (*right*).

A French late 19th-century ivory and silver purse. The purse is hinged and has a finely wrought clasp; its concertina interior with central lift fastening is lined with turquoise moiré silk.

FASHIONABLE CONSTRAINT

The fashionable S-bend silhouette so favored by women in the early years of the 20th century was typified by an exaggerated curve of the back, a pigeon breast, and a narrow waist. Although women were dressed in layers of soft lingerie and ruffled lace that made them look helplessly feminine, underneath, their torsos were rigidly corseted. Skirts fitted closely over the hips and flared out to brush the ground, while bodices were high collared, waists tight and belted, and cuffs and collars ornately embellished. Parisian fashions were dominant, copied in both the United States and Britain, where King Edward VII's love of the lavish style of the *Belle Epoque* in France lent power to the influence of Paris, especially after his ascent to the British throne in 1901.

Dress was a focus of femininity and a demonstration of the affluence and taste of the leisured upper classes. There were different dress styles for all manner of occasions; dresses made of dark blue voile and colored satin were considered suitable for seaside promenades, while those in delicate white or ivory cottons were deemed more suitable for afternoon tea dances. On summer afternoons ladies of fashion wore white lace and organdy dresses with high collars and long, tight sleeves, a nostalgic image of long lost summers, in part borne out by photographs of the time.

Accessories of all kinds accompanied these elegant, extravagant dresses, the fair complexion of their wearers protected from the sun by delicate parasols of fine silk net, tulle, ribbons, and silk flowers. Shoes and stockings were relatively plain, and revealed only intermittently beneath ankle-length skirts as a woman walked, but hats were especially important. A greater emphasis was placed upon them than any other accessory, and by 1910 they were enormous and ornate, adorned with feathers, flowers, ribbons, lace, and even stuffed birds. In winter, hats of fur or velvet were matched by massive muffs of the same material, many of which had pockets inside or an attached matching purse.

This delicate metal chatelaine bag was worn hung from the waist by a short chain. The main body of the bag is plain and composed of flat metal links, edged with small beads. The top lid is worked in fine detail and features a filigree butterfly, its body and wings inset with turquoise. The inside of the lid is inset with an oval mirror with gold surround.

Bags Remain Small

In comparison with hats, bags were very small, and purses even smaller, but there was a reason for this. Just as the exaggeratedly large hat beautifully framed a woman's face, so an extremely small bag drew attention to her well-cared-for hands and slender wrists, emphasizing that this was a true lady of leisure. Any bag larger than the daintiest reticule would be carried by a man or a porter, as a woman seen carrying her own bag would be taken for a member of a lower social class.

Early in the century, bags were held in the hand or hung from a belt. Many were so small that there was barely room inside them for the tips of the fingers, and in some cases, a purse could be even smaller than the tassels on the cuffs of a daytime dress. What exactly it was designed to hold is a mystery.

A general confusion of ribbons, flowers, braiding, and tassels smothered the surface of most bags, which were generally held by a cord, sometimes wound several times around a gloved wrist or finger. A society woman would change her outfit and accessories several times a day, and traveling, visiting, indoor occasions, and formal occasions all required different styles of bag.

As the manufacture of handbags became more sophisticated, bag interiors were often carefully compartmentalized for specific functions. Many were intricately crafted into bags for visiting, which incorporated a visiting card case and pencil, a perfume bottle, and a purse big enough to hold a few coins, or the combined purse and card case, among the most upscale versions of which was a bag of powder-blue crushed morocco leather mounted in silver and decorated with beautifully enameled pheasants in natural colors.

As upper-class women never used public transportation but traveled by chauffeur-driven car or hansom cab, they carried very little money. The maid or butler made front door keys unnecessary, and make-up beyond a dab of powder was generally regarded as risqué, so bags were not designed to hold much more than a powder puff (although make-up was probably much more widely used than generally admitted.) As a result, bags for the upper classes remained small and decorative rather than practical for quite some time, and many opted for the chatelaine bag suspended from a metal belt.

The Advent of the Evening Bag

Early in the century, evening bags were often made in the drawstring style, ornately decorated with rich embroidery and beadwork on velvet and satin. The original, softly gathered drawstring Dorothy, or

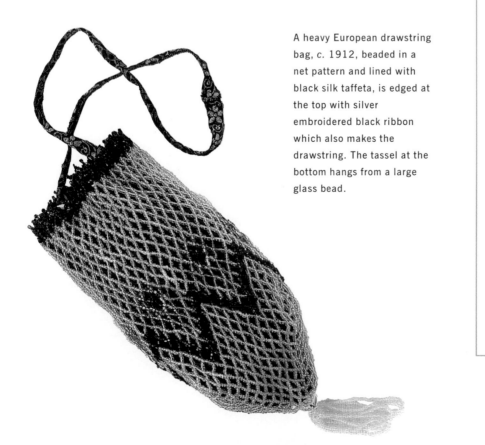

A heavy European drawstring bag, c. 1912, beaded in a net pattern and lined with black silk taffeta, is edged at the top with silver embroidered black ribbon which also makes the drawstring. The tassel at the bottom hangs from a large glass bead.

The appeal of the chatelaine

The custom for hanging useful household objects from a belt around the waist first became popular with women in the 17th century, but enjoyed numerous revivals thereafter. The above English chatelaine purse is made from black velvet lined with black silk and mounted on a silver frame, and was attached to a chatelaine or chain belt by a ring. In November 1911, chatelaines were described as "essentially feminine and housewifely" by the American magazine *McCall's*, which noted that, "Today milady carries her keys and purse, her handkerchief and vanity box in a reticule so necessary that it has become a part of her costume." Almost anything that swung attractively from a belt, drawing attention to a narrow waist, was worn, including watches hung from long chains that tucked into the belt or a special pocket, perfume bottles, and chatelaine "swan" pens, first produced in 1902 from chased silver.

As chatelaines were thought to be useful both inside and outside the house — not only were they decorative, but they also left the hands free to carry a parasol or muff, or to manage the long skirts of the day — chatelaine accessories were much collected, and were often suggested by women's magazines as suitable Christmas gifts. Many of these items were later to be carried in a handbag.

Large handbags and hats were very much à la mode in 1910. Cartoon from *Punch* Magazine, London.

SLAVES OF FASHION.

Ethel. "Lend me your hanky, Mabel." *Mabel.* "Haven't you one in your bag?"
Ethel. "Good gracious, my dear girl, do you think I should put anything in this bag? It's as much as I can carry empty!"

Dorcas, bag, dating from around 1880, was a practical but homey affair, far from the high fashion item it was to become. But before long, the Dorothy was appearing in any number of sophisticated guises, embroidered with steel beads, lined with silk, and with a beveled mirror forming the base of the interior.

A pretty French Dorothy-style beaded bag, *c.* 1910, made of colored glass beads on a canvas backing, and lined with turquoise cotton.

Metal Bags

Metal was a fashionable material for both evening and day bags. Some of the most desirable examples were made from a lattice work chain of gold over gold-colored silk. These were then studded with precious stones such amethysts, pearls, or turquoise, or their paste equivalents. There were steel chain bags, too, in the same latticework design lined with silver gray silk, while at the more expensive end of the market, "fish scale" bags and purses of silver mesh were popular, many with substantial silver tops. Gold chain purse ensembles with a gold bracelet and gold cluster pencil set with gems were also highly sought. Plain metal open-mesh bags were enlivened by colored silk or suede linings; although these looked attractive, they tended to wear out quickly and had to be replaced frequently. Many such bags and purses were made in Germany, and exported throughout Europe and North America.

Specially designed theater and opera bags were made commercially, many in the various shades of dyed suede which had recently become available. These were fitted out with all an operagoer could require, the most expensive examples containing opera glasses, a fan, purse, mirror, writing tablet, and even a powder puff made of swan's-down. In some, glass bottles for smelling salts or perfume were also included.

A once striking steel-framed evening bag (left) of midnight blue velvet, set with steel beads in a floral pattern, C. 1915–18, but now sadly rusted. Probably French, it still retains a silk backed inside mirror, a push-button tope, and velvet pulling tab.

Practical and sturdy brown leather bag, with a metal frame, c. 1890, used for traveling.

An early 20th-century bag depicting a rural scene with cottages, a stream, and ducks in multicolored beadwork. Embedded with semiprecious stones, the frame includes a tiny duck motif on the top left.

Bags to Fit an Expanding Lifestyle

In the early 1900s, as the occupations and expectations of women changed, they began to go out more. Although a lot of shopping was still paid for on account and delivered to the home, large, capacious leather bags specifically referred to as shopping bags began to appear. These were an extension of the practical leather bags on metal or wooden frames which had been available for some years, as accompaniments to other types of leather baggage used for motor car and train travel. These leather "handbags" remained with the traveler — as opposed to the rest of the baggage, which was stowed elsewhere — and by 1900, they had become as indispensable to many women as they are to this day.

Many boxlike leather handbags were very small at the turn of the century and were considered fashionable accessories for tailored outfits, their neat lines echoing the smooth, fitted costumes of the day, carried between thumb and index finger by a loop handle. They were often miniaturized versions of large suitcases and bags, and generally retained the stylistic details of larger pieces of baggage, such as reinforced metal corners and numerous complicated fastenings.

One disadvantage of the handbag was that it provided a great opportunity for the thief, who quickly turned from pickpocket to bag snatcher. Safety catches and locking systems were a preoccupation of handbag manufacturers and a key selling feature;

The fashionable S-shape is clear in these early illustrations for paper patterns of ladies' traveling suits. The skirts are heavily gathered, tucked and bowed to exaggerate the hips and accentuate the cinched-in waist. Umbrellas, chatelaines and reticules complete the turn of the century picture.

Turning to the East

In 1910, Serge Diaghilev brought his Ballet Russe to Europe, and his production of *Scheherazade* had an enormous impact on fashion, especially in its use of bright, resounding color and fantastic costumes. As early as 1911, the designs of the French couturier Paul Poiret reflected these influences.

The fascination with Orientalism found its way into designs of beaded and embroidered handbags. Embroidered Oriental scenes and rich brocaded bags with carved and pierced mounts of ivory were very fashionable, while the finishing touch on a bag of rich black faille, complete with a case for paper money, puff, and mirror, was its mounting, made of real ivory and carved in the form of three elephants.

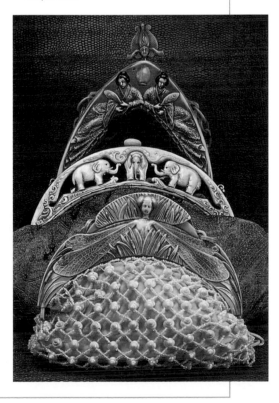

Beaded bags

The heyday of the glass beaded bag was in the early 1920s, when most were made in Czechoslovakia and Germany, and decorated with Bohemian and Bavarian glass beads. Much of the beadwork was multipatterned, and took its early designs from tapestry work and petit-point embroidery, each bead resembling a stitch in floral or scenic patterns and views. Although some beaded bags were simple Dorothy shapes, others were mounted on ornate metal frames with a chain. Many were exported to England and the United States. from France, where quantities of cut-steel bags, with each tiny bead of cut steel sewn on by hand, were also produced. The fringed mesh and bead evening bag (*below*, Linda Bee) with a metal frame is probably French, *c. 1910*.

Stylized fruit and bows in soft blues and greys with pink and red accents adorn the steel-framed, beaded bag (*left*) of European origin.

evening bags also had gilt frames with the latest in safety clasps. But despite the attention they must have attracted from pickpockets, purses attached to the outside of the bag became a brief fashion fad, as were outside flap pockets on leather bags. In 1912, Dorothy bags in black or colored velvet were being made with small outside purses, while in other cases, they were attached to the main bag by chains.

Capitalizing on Advanced Leather Production

Handbag manufacturers quickly responded to industrial developments in leather production, and particularly in the area of aniline dyeing processes. Tanneries often sent their leather to be dyed abroad, mainly to Germany, where such industrial processes were highly advanced. Morocco, calf, sealskin, and all shades of dyed leather were used to make bags, and before long more sophisticated dyeing and embossing techniques led to the arrival of imitation leathers, which were treated to resemble more expensive hides.

These imitation leathers were used in endless bag designs, including handbags with flap fronts that were known as "avenue" or "boulevard" bags, and which looked remarkably modern. The flap, which was sometimes a double flap for extra security, fastened at the front with gilt button fasteners, and the corners of the bag were protected with gilt metal. The bag itself opened under the flap with a twist of the interlocking ball knobs. These bags were designed to be held by short straps, attached to the top or back of the bag, or simply tucked under the arm, so anticipating the flat, envelope-like pochette of 1915.

THE NEW SILHOUETTE

After 1907, the new Directoire fashions came into vogue, featuring narrower skirts, higher waists, and asymmetrical drapes. As skirt lengths rose, shoes, button boots, and silk stockings became more significant, and fur was used as a decorative trimming on hems and cuffs as well as for muffs and stoles. Hats were smaller and often trimmed with egret feathers, reinforcing the slender look emphasized by the Paris fashions of 1910 onwards. Fashion illustrations became more animated, with scarves trailing and skirts blowing — a reflection of the increasing speed of life as the automobile and the train made traveling faster — and clothes and accessories were generally more fluent and less inhibiting to movement. One exception was Paul Poiret's hobble skirt of 1910, worn with an accompanying fashion for enormous bags, a fashion that attracted public ridicule at the time. Chic walking suits influenced by men's tailoring were much more typical of the era.

These were generally accompanied by fabric bags with long cords and tassels, while Dorothy bags made of soft fabrics with beading or embroidered with fringing were seen at a variety of social events, from the theater to horse race meets. The bag was generally attached to a long silk cord looped over the wrist and hung at knee level. Fabric Dorothy bags were often made by dressmakers as part of a matching outfit, and one fashion illustration of 1901 showing a lace and sequin robe with matching drawstring or Dorothy bag set a trend which enterprising local dressmakers with an eye for Parisian fashions swiftly followed.

Finding Relief in Frivolity

There was a slowing down of fashion developments in 1914, the first year of World War I. During the war years, skirts were shorter and fuller, and although charity shows to support the French fashion industry were held in New York, the French government put restrictions on overt displays of rich clothes and jewelry.

In Britain, too, the old ways began to change as servants left, never to return. For the first time, the elegant tailored suit worn by society women was put to use — one fashion commentator noted in November 1917 that "it will directly appeal to the busy woman who has relinquished her maid" — and as the war progressed, military details crept into women's fashions. Boots got higher, and handbag straps shorter.

The design of the interiors of bags was increasingly dictated by developments in the cosmetics and beauty industry. Make-up was no longer frowned upon in quite the same way, and bag manufacturers began to recognize a woman's desire to carry it with her. The number of compartments inside handbags increased, and a further

A sliver mesh bag with an ornate silver frame, short chain, and finger ring. There are three chained attachments: perfume flagon, compact, and card case. Also shown is a double-ended miser's purse in silver mesh with twist knobs. Both are turn of the century German bags.

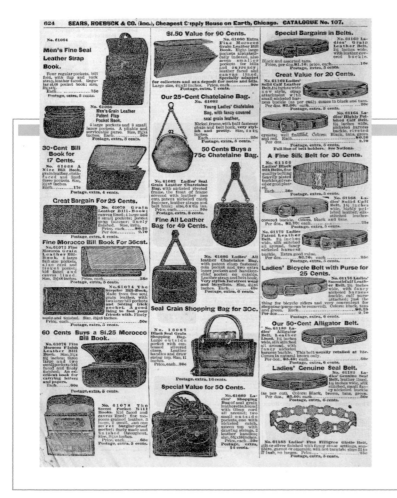

The Sears, Roebuck prototype

Although the idea was relatively new, the variety of leather handbags on sale to the public by 1900 was extensive. The extent of the range available can be seen in a catalog of that year from the leading American mail order company, Sears, Roebuck. In it, a variety of styles and sizes are shown decorated with fancy embossed work in floral patterns. Many of the bags contained pockets, and some a matching purse, card case, and mirror. Their metal frames were opened by twist ball knobs or a push lock, and they were carried by short leather strap handles which hung over the arm or were held in the hand.

industry in miniature handbag accessories sprang up. Vanity bags in black moiré, lined with white, and fitted with small gilt manicure cases became fashionable, while others made in black and white corded silk contained gilt cases that held a pencil, nail file, and button hook. (The button hook was used for fastening the side-buttoned boots that were worn at the time, and which were beginning to be revealed by rising skirt lengths.)

The wide adoption of cigarette smoking by both men and women was also noted by bag manufacturers, who began to produce models expressly to cater to the habit, such as combined pigskin cases for check book, cigarettes, money, cards, stamps, and other similar uses. The walletlike case was customized to reflect the new social habits of both men and women.

Luxury Prevails

But accessories were one way to raise the spirits, and some firms continued to make luxurious bags during the war years, including the British bag specialist John Pound & Co. Its bags made from morocco, seal, and crocodile leathers, and advertised in 1914, were shown open to reveal exquisite interiors as well as an attractive outside. The short stirrup handle was first seen in 1916 on bags such as those sold by Dickins and Jones, the London department store, while another well-known London store, Liberty's, sold tasseled Dorothy bags in velvet and silk.

Silver or gold gauze tissue dance bags, outlined with matching metal lace, were also fashionable, adorned with tiny fruits or flowers and with mirror bases. And bags of colored silk were made with separate accessories, such as nail files or polish, a powder puff, a mirror, or a trinket box, all decorated with the fashionable dainty French ribbon and lace embroideries.

Fur Finds a Market

Between 1910 and 1920, fur was still prized despite its cost, and its wear was not confined to the winter months. Coats were voluminous and unfitted, and automobile coats often had integral pockets. One such was an Erté design for a

The charming French chatelaine purse (*right*), beaded in a multicolored floral pattern, was attached to the chatelaine by a small ring. A silver 3-D bit, dated 1911, was found inside.

The rise of the home-made bag

In the early 1900s, home dressmaking was enjoying a boom. As mass-produced sewing machines became more affordable, the related trade in paper patterns expanded.

Reticules and Dorothy bags were accessories that could be made at home, requiring little more expertise than that which most well brought-up young women already had at their fingertips. Countless soft drawstring bags were made, some to be used as receptacles for knitting or embroidery, others as handbags. More ornate versions were considered appropriate for both day and evening wear, while larger cloth versions ideally suited the new Directoire fashions. Complete kits for producing very professional-looking bags were sold through many magazines, which also featured patterns and other ideas for hand work. Cross-stitch embroidery, beading, crochet, and tatting, all widely practiced hobbies of the day, were incorporated into bag designs, and silver and tortoiseshell frame tops could be bought separately. The white silk drawstring bag (*above*, Steinberg & Tolkien, London) was probably home-made. Embroidered and appliqued on both sides with a floral design, it is lined with pink silk and has a matching ribbon drawstring. Although much repaired, the bag is still very pretty. Such "fancy work" was regarded as a suitable occupation for leisured women, for whom these restful pursuits helped to pass the time. But the vogue for home-made bags went out of style once there were more important matters to think about, with the onset of World War I.

A pochette-like French snakeskin bag (*above*) c. 1900, features a finely carved ivory panel in shallow relief.

Silver, zig-zag patterned mesh bag (*left*) of the early 1900s with contrasting tassle.

Crocodile-skin effect markings decorate this hallmark silver English finger purse of 1912 (*below*), which has a central shield bearing the initials MB. It closes with a twist knob clasp and small chains link to a finger ring.

chamois and seal coat with a collection of tiny flap pockets with snap fastenings to hold make-up and trinkets.

Fur muffs, many with inside pockets, were also popular, although women often carried fur muffs in conjunction with handbags decorated with fur in imaginative ways. One example on sale in 1912 at Mappin and Webb in London was made from beaded black velvet mounted with three ermine skins, the tails forming natural tassels that were echoed by silk tassels at the sides of the bag. Ermine tails formed the fringe and handles of a very modern bag designed by Erté in October 1918, a design that made the most of the fad for furs such as fox, ermine, musquash (a.k.a.muskrat), sable, raccoon, mink, seal, skunk, monkey, beaver, pony, and wolf. Fur was often combined with other materials, with bags made with bits of fur left over from a collar or a renovated coat, and the fad even spread to knitting bags.

Couture Takes Over the Handbag

By December 1919, top Parisian couture designers such as Martial et Armand and Paul Poiret were turning their attention to accessories. Brocades, silver lace, ornamented leather, fur, lace, and innumerable combinations were used with mountings of tortoiseshell, ivory, old gold, silver, and gilt to produce a selection of handbags that were truly impressive. From this point on, the handbag became an indispensable part of a woman's fashion ensemble, as important as her shoes, hat, and gloves. The sheer diversity and range of handbags available would mean that every woman, from every level of society, would carry a handbag, a trend that has not changed in the ensuing eighty years.

Picking Up the Pieces
of the Jazz Age Pattern

The Roaring Twenties came in with a bang and with the decade came revolutionary changes to society and to accepted social conventions. It was also a decade of revolutionary change for all aspects of fashion and design, and bags were no exception. They reflected the Art Deco style of the period: bright and light, extravagant and eyecatching, often made of brocade and generously adorned with glitter, embroidery, and beading. In the aftermath of World War I, the atmosphere in Europe was inevitably gloomy, in stark contrast to that of the sunlit, innocent era before war broke out. In spite of the fact that many women had lost loved ones, the war was a catalyst for change in the emancipation of women. During the war years, women developed a taste for life outside the confines of the domestic environment, and refused to return to the status quo once the conflict was over. The situation was exacerbated by the shortage of eligible young men, due to the huge loss of life in the trenches, and women remained unmarried in unprecedented numbers. These countless women now had to earn their own living.

The Easter Parade in Atlantic City provided an opportunity for young women to show off their spring finery. New cloche hats and long flowing dresses are accessorized with scarves, fur collars, and envelope clutch bags.

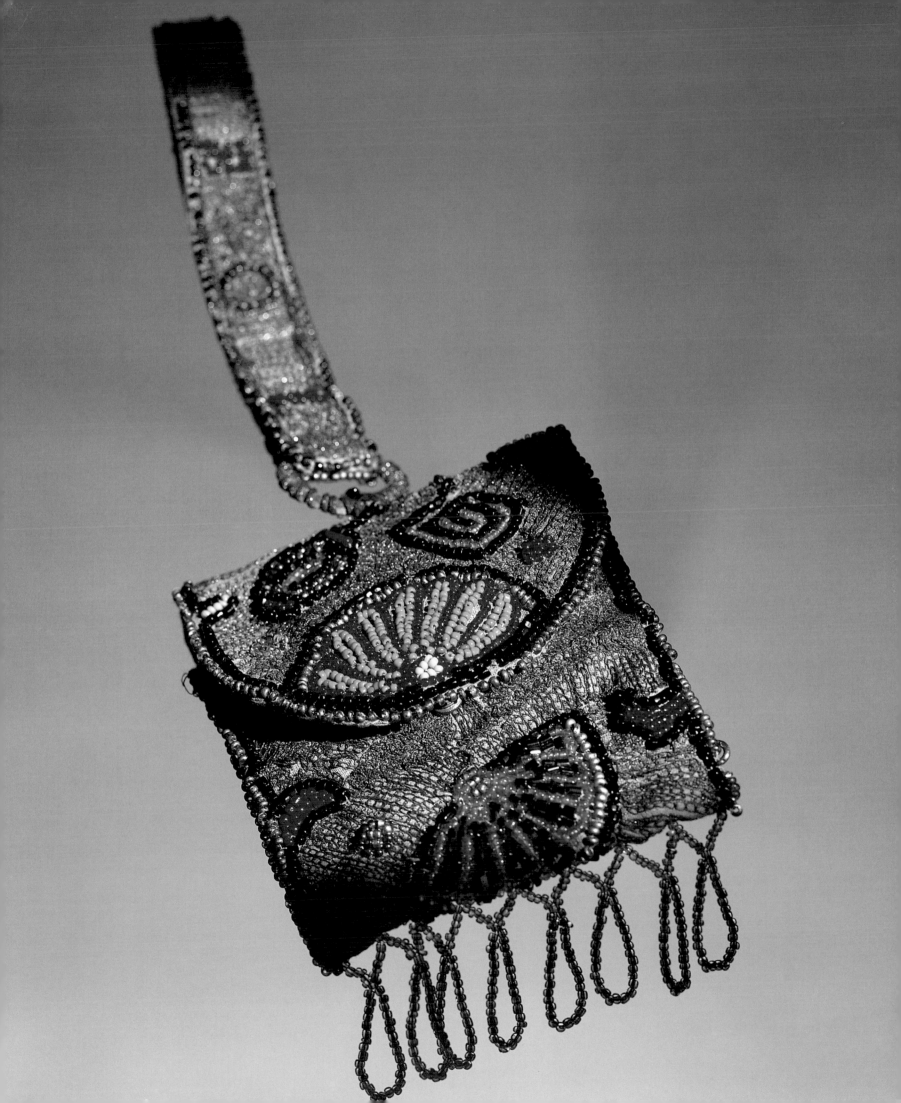

A 1920s evening bag made from lengths of silk taffeta ribbon in orange and blue, stitched into a circular flower shape. Lined with turquoise fabric, it features a circular mirror attached to the bag.

A NEW AMERICAN CULTURE

The devastation of war had not affected the economies on the other side of the Atlantic as it had in much of Europe. Despite the huge fatalities among troops sent overseas, industrial and financial developments in the United States led to a dynamic period of growth. Although the United States still looked to Paris for the latest in haute couture, and ordered many of its fashionable goods from continental Europe, it developed a massive manufacturing industry of its own. Thanks to its many talented designers, a distinctive American style was beginning to emerge.

American culture influenced European films, music, and dance crazes, but for the uppercrust English aristocrats such as the American-born Nancy, Lady Astor, dresses were still bought in Paris and tailored suits in London. Hats still had wide brims, many made of straw or tulle, and tied with lace veils, but as the decade progressed, the cloche shape dominated, decorated with appliqué or banded with contrasting ribbon. Bandeaus of patterned silk were also considered stylish, tied around the forehead.

Although strict dress codes still existed, styles were changing rapidly and becoming more democratic. Fewer layers of clothing were worn and undergarments became far less restrictive as boned corsets were abandoned. The physical freedom this allowed the modern woman was reflected in the simple clothes and functional accessories of the day, which incorporated the dynamic, progressive new styles so prevalent in wider design.

Living It Up in Peacetime
By 1920, the bag had become a fashionable necessity and an extremely varied adjunct to the feminine toilette. The leisured classes owned as many styles of bag as there were hours in the day: bags for town use might be an antelope bag with tortoiseshell fastening; for shopping, some torpedo-shaped examples made of seal; for evening wear, a bag with pocketcases of black and silver lamé; and for dances, a bag made out of Japanese silk.

A glance at the contents of a woman's bag revealed some of the social changes that had taken place since the turn of the century. Face powder, eye make-up, and lipstick were all carried, sometimes in special make-up holders and daringly applied in public, as were plastic vanity bags hinged like deep powder compacts. Bobbed hair combs sold by the American company Sears, Roebuck through their mail order catalogs reflected the latest hair style.

Cigarette smoking was more widely practised than ever, generating a

A *minaudière*-style evening bag which holds make-up and small change. Probably French, the chrome body is covered in richly printed leather and has a badly worn leather handle. The interior is luxurious, lined in brown silk and beautifully fitted with lined pockets and a mirror.

whole range of new accessories manufactured out of metal, tortoiseshell, leather, ivory, and plastic. Cigarette cases and lighters, containers for safety matches, and coordinated long cigarette holders were either carried in bags as separate accessories or formed customized compartments within the interiors of smart bags.

At night, small, rigid vanity cases for make-up and toiletries were often carried to accompany sleeveless evening dresses with low cut backs. Many of these vanity cases were French, molded in new plastics such as celluloid and imitation ivory, and lined with the new fabric rayon viscose, which was also used for fabric bags. Tiny lipstick-shaped dance reticules were fashionable in 1921, made out of celluloid and inset with paste. These were held by a short silk cord and were designed to contain rouge, powder, and lipstick, hidden behind a large tassel.

Long strings of beads and dangling earrings were generally worn with evening dresses, although make-up accessories also doubled as jewelry from time to time. Solid silver powder puff and lipstick holders not much bigger than the lipsticks themselves were worn around the neck on fine chains, while silver vanity boxes with mirror and powder puff were suspended on wrist chains. The owner's name was engraved on many. Silver mesh bags were also popular, many with a mirror and powder puff set into the top, and on some, novelty silver "powderettes" shook powder onto the puff in the same way as a sugar shaker.

New Designs For New Materials

In keeping with the trend for simpler clothing, skirts were shorter than they had even been by 1925. Smart, tailored two piece day suits and the simple pleated jersey skirts and cardigans, created by the renowned French designer Coco Chanel, were accompanied by flat, envelope type bags known as pochettes. It was Chanel who introduced clothes made with

The tiny lipstick shaped dance reticule (*above*) made of celluloid depicts several of the dominant 1920s themes. Made of the new modern material of the time, celluloid was a plastic that could be molded into innovative shapes with smooth, rounded edges, and it could be hinged and compartmentalized inside for make-up and perfume. Black was a popular and stylish color and the long silk cords and large tassels were other popular features of the period.

The sporting accessory

Social sporting events, such as horse race meets or rowing regattas, encouraged their own tailormade accessories. Race-card notecases made of leather were commonplace, while a combined race-card handbag of 1929 would have held a race-card, pencil, a notebook, a purse, and a mirror.

Women no longer had outfits just for social occasions, however. Sporting activities demanded their own special costumes, and casual, soft, drawstring Dorothy bags to match were very much in use for bathing and other such pursuits. Typical of 1921 was a large, polka dot drawstring bag with deep ruff, illustrated with a coordinated bathing outfit in a magazine of the day. The waterproof bag was probably made of rubberized fabric, which was by then generally available. Tennis sweaters with enormous lattice work pockets in which to carry tennis balls were another fashionable accessory in the early 1920s. Not all women had such a range of social opportunities, however, and many survived with far fewer bags.

This Art Deco handbag, *c.* 1920–30, has a gilt frame with twist-knob fastening and a fine chain handle. It is soft pink, finely embroidered with a gold vermicular pattern.

quilted fabrics — quilted bags were made to match — and dresses and coats covered with pockets. In the early 1920s, voile dresses with appliqué petals or handkerchief points inspired by French designer Madeleine Vionnet were highly fashionable; these were worn with highheeled bar shoes and hair cropped daringly short and styled close to the head. Gathered bags whose petal shaped ruffs echoed the dress were seen everywhere. Printed fabrics were also in demand, as was rayon, the new fabric being produced in America. Rayon was generally used as a silk substitute, though its potential as a good stocking material was beginning to be realized. Patent leather, another new material, was introduced in 1927, while advances to the zipper had an impact on all aspects of fashion.

At night, the beaded, swinging dance dresses which symbolized the dynamic 'flapper' look were dressed up with trimmings of black monkey fur and feathers. Handbags were also beaded, many geometrically patterned, and under the influence of current trends in art, including decorative art designs shown at the 1925 Art Deco exhibition in Paris, Cubism and the German design movement, Bauhaus. While handbags were hung on short straps and opened with geometrically shaped clasps, the streamlined pochette, soon seen everywhere, was held briskly under the arm.

Luxury, Both Real and Fake

Luxurious leather handbags and traveling goods were made by upscale firms such as Cartier's of Bond Street, London. One "fascinating novelty" advertised in 1925 was a traveling dressing case which also served as a dressing table. Part of its lid formed a hinged flap containing a large mirror, while on either side were compartments that held brushes, a manicure set, powder boxes, scent bottles, and other accessories. The new "strip fastener," or zipper, was recommended as a particularly secure feature. Despite the pockets on Chanel's jersey cardigans and motoring coats — and curios such as a 1923 beige suede scarf with places for

A bold, beaded foliage design against black and brown stripes adorns a French 1920s bag (*right*), with a rounded Bakelite frame.

This unusual metal evening purse of the 1920s (*left*) has an octagonal top and chain mesh body, culminating in a gold tassel. The top is patterned in a floral Art Nouveau design.

Probably French, this black (fading to brown) antelope suede evening bag has a silver frame with a bold design of marcasite and cornelian. Made in the late 1920s, the bag has a pocket, mirror case, and purse inside.

A movie still from the 1920s, clearly illustrates the glamorous flapper style of the period. Handkerchief point hems, long strings of pearls, close cropped hair, and gathered bags holding make-up and cigarettes completed the flapper image.

powder and rouge — the closer fitting clothes of the period meant that larger handbags were essential. The traditional framed bag was still widely seen, although the shape became more pouched and rounded at the base as the decade progressed, the fabric or soft leather gathered or pleated into large curved frames.

A typical bag of 1921 was made from black faille silk, with an inner pocket, and rounded mount of 'simuli', or imitation, tortoiseshell. Frames or simulated materials such as this — known in America as 'shell' rather than the English 'simuli' — were much cheaper than the real thing. Other flatter, squarer styles of bag were attached to straight metal frames, and were embroidered or appliquéd in abstract patterns inspired by Art Deco. For a more formal occasion, silk embroidery was prevalent, with highly decorated mounts. Most bags had short carrying straps or chains, or a wide fabric strap to slip the hand through.

INSPIRATION FROM AFAR

The discovery of King Tutankhamen's tomb in 1922 triggered a widespread fascination with Egyptian motifs and patterns, and hieroglyphics and scarabs covered all manner of decorative objects and accessories, including handbags. Typical of the trend was a matching cloche hat and large flat bag made from a richly colored piece of oriental embroidery, decorated with a sphinx and palm tree design by Sybil Pendlebury and illustrated in Vogue in 1925. African jewelry and fabrics were another enthusiasm and the Revue Nègre in Paris starring Josephine Baker shocked and delighted everyone. One magazine in

This simple pochette, c. 1925, has unusual double flaps which provide the perfect canvas for a "Chinese" scene of mountains, boats, and pagodas in embossed and brightly painted leather. As a finishing touch, the elephant tabs are carved from ivory.

A sumptuous English evening clutch bag from the late 1920s made of dark green velvet and lined with cream moiré silk. The striking rhinestone clasp adds a further touch of glamor.

1920 showed a scarf and tasseled Dorothy bag in matching African patterned fabric, and another illustrated a 1928 bag made from a Bessarabian prayer rug. For a short time fashion devotees diligently made raffia work bags with primitive figurative patterns at home.

Chinese brocade bags were recommended as desirable presents for Christmas 1921, some made of imitation ivory and others with ostrich feathers reinforced with black silk cords and tassels. Costing a great deal more, but very fashionable in 1921 were magnificent handbags made of antique Chinese embroideries with large ornate frames and mounts carved from ivory tusks. The length of the frame was covered in tiny figures carved in great detail, while the lift clasp to open the bags was made from a real *netsuke*, or carved Japanese toggle. A comparable bag in black and gold brocade topped with the then fashionable *netsuke* in solid ivory was available from J. C. Vickery's of London for day and evening use. Imitation ivory frames made of plastic were obviously much cheaper.

Bags With Humor

Novelty bags were another feature of the 1920s, the trend starting with those sketched by Erté for *Harper's Bazaar* in June 1921. Intriguingly headed "The fragile bisque doll finds a new role," the feature showed delightful doll bags, perfectly dressed in the latest fashions, and with their full skirts forming the bag. With their

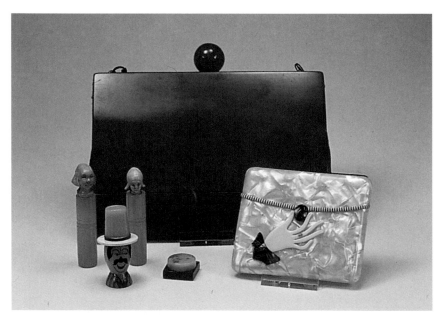

Red plastic bag is bold and bright with a round knob clasp and simple parallel lines at the base. The small molded pochette features a hand opening the clasp, a popular contemporary motif. Both bags were made in the early 1920s.

painted features and dresses of silver tissue and taffetta, embellished with semiprecious stones, the doll bags were carried on thin chains as a complement to the larger outfit. Some women mimicked the dolls' outfits in their own attire.

Other novelty bags of the early 1920s included "floral bags" made of silk flowers. These were sometimes exceptionally beautiful, imitating such flowers as orchids in accurate detail, and were carried in the hand or pinned to the corsage. On the whole, they resembled nosegays arranged to surround the inner receptacle, and some contained the extra novelty of a powder puff in a silk bag with a tiny mirror set into the heart of a flower. Jays in Regent Street, London, sold butterfly-shaped creations in shot taffetas, richly embroidered with iridescent sequins and beads, and pretty rose bags formed from velvet and satin "petals" were also available. Curious glove purses from France consisted of a glove in embroidered white suede and an integral, long purse which fell from the wrist and ended in a tassel, holding at most a handkerchief and a lipstick. Equally bizarre bags disguised as small dogs were sold to Harrods customers in 1927, complete with fluffy white tail and red ribbons.

Extravagant Evening Accessories

In the 1920s, evening bags came in a multitude of materials. There were fabric Dorothy bags, bags of metal mesh and beaded bags. Cartier constructed expensive drawstring bags from the softest leather which was gathered accordion style, while the Gazette du Bon Ton

This beaded tortoise shaped bag has feet and head made in mottled tortoiseshell, and beadwork beautifully worked in browns, black, and gold to resemble the markings on the shell. A brown silk grosgrain ribbon serves as a wrist strap.

The significance of the zipper

Although the zipper did not make its mark on bag design until the 1920s, it was not a new invention. The first "slide fastener" was registered in Chicago in 1893 by its inventor Whitcomb L. Judson, in spite of the fact that it was a Swede, Dr. Gideon Sundback, who first managed to attach interlocking metal hooks to a flexible fabric background. The zipper acquired its name at a promotional lunch for the product in 1926, when the novelist Gilbert Frankau is said to have declared, "Zip! It's open. Zip! It's closed."

featured tiny evening bags in sharp, modern shapes in 1922. One was round and quite flat, to be held by the tassel, while another was fixed to a round silver bangle, and was worn on the wrist.

Framed evening bags often had highly decorated and jeweled metal mounts, their ornate metal chains set with beads. Amber and tortoiseshell were favored materials, as were marcasite clasps and marcasite monograms. The silver mesh bags seen early in the decade fell from favor, although enameled mesh bags enjoyed a brief revival in America in 1929. They were rarely found in Europe, however.

Bags embroidered both by hand and by machine made a comeback in the late 1920s in silk embroidered floral designs, tapestry and petit-point work, Chinese and Oriental silk embroidery, and French *cordeaux* or cord work. Liberty of London sold hand-embroidered petit point bags with an amazing 1500 stitches to the square inch (2 sq cm), each of which apparently took four months to make.

Elegant Day Bags

Leather framed bags for smart day wear were made from reptile skins such as snake, lizard, python, and alligator. A lizard skin model by Hermes illustrated in the *Gazette du Bon Ton* in 1924–25 showed a new elegance. Triangular at the base, the bag's frame was concealed and its single handle was slim and short, and centred

Slim, blue satin 1920s evening bag, probably English, is covered in regularly placed rhinestone studs, while the shaped frame has intricate Art Nouveau style metal work and rhinestone edging. It opens with a large cut glass bead clasp, and the slender metal chain is decorated with cut glass beads as well.

Red leather bag with its smooth metal clasp is beautifully patterned with vertical lines inlaid in blue, yellow, and green leather. Made in Austria, *c.* 1925, by Wiener Werkstatte, famous for its jewelry, furniture, and cutlery. This bag is attributed to designer Josef Hoffman.

A 1920s celluloid evening vanity would be carried over the finger at dances, and held the bare essentials — lipstick and powder. The turquoise color of this one is unusual; it is inset with rhinestones and the cord and tassel are silk.

above the neat lift clasp. Across the Channel, the new shapes found in London were taller than they were wide. One retailer, Mappin and Webb, sold models fashioned from blue crocodile, green pleated morocco with an onyx and marcasite mount, and fawn seal with a gilt frame and colored stone mount at the top. Softer leathers, such as antelope and suede, were gathered into mounts of lacquer and eggshell.

After 1926, bags became completely circular, or else very wide and pouched, with enormous mounts of marcasite and jade almost as big as the pouch itself. But the epitome of the 1920s handbag was the clutch bag, or pochette. These had been introduced before the decade started, but soon became the most dominant and stylish of all bag shapes. The pochette, designed to be carried under the arm, demonstrated an assertiveness and sense of purpose that was captured in contemporary photographs and drawings of women. Indeed in 1924, *Vogue* satirized the American tourist as arriving in France with a large, gathered frame handbag but returning to America with a neat, sharp pochette tucked tightly under her arm.

Although early pochettes had a flap or envelope front, later models came with a zippered top, which did not need a flap. Most had no handles or a small handstrap at the back, and were smart and simple, in line with the neatness and simplicity of the

Beaded bags with flapper dresses

Sumptuous and multicolored bead bags used for both dress and shopping were regarded as stylish for most of the 1920s, and especially those with Oriental colorings and motifs that were so popular in all the arts. In 1925, beads and thread embroideries were elaborate and brilliant, smothering entire bags and even dresses, as well as being used as trimmings. Some bags were beaded in traditional floral patterns that would not have been out of place ten years earlier, while those with abstract patterns matched the beaded dance dresses of the 1920s flappers. The small purse (*right*) beaded in black and green glass beads in stripes with a floral motif picked out in red, pink, and yellow, is a typical example of the traditional floral pattern that was so popular.

Made in Scotland in 1920, this bag may have been adapted from a sporran. A curved, engraved silver frame supports a tooled leather bag covered with fur.

Dunhill lights the way

Most unusual of all 1920s bags were the 'Lytup' handbags of 1922, made in England by Alfred Dunhill, the sole manufacturer. Made in satin or printed chiffon velvet with a carved plastic frame, a little electric light automatically switched on when the handbag was opened to help the owner find her keys or money. It was also designed to help when using the bag's fitted mirror wherever the lights were dim, as in a taxi.

new clothes fashions. It also provided an ideal focus for decorative images or abstract patterns, and rectangular pochettes with matching hats started to appear, decorated with patterns formed from insets and appliqué in Art Deco styles.

Decorating the Pochette

Exotic leathers were used to make pochettes, from black antelope inset with braid, brown suede with insets of snakeskin, and shagreen strapped in tan calf. Washable, glossy patent leather pochettes for spring and summer emerged in the late 1920s, while 1928 evening pochettes in silver rhinestones, from J. C. Vickery in London, had a "jazz" design in brown, mauve, and red brilliants. Others were embroidered in zigzag patterns of gold and silk braid.

"Novel purses," thicker pochettes shaped like books, were introduced by Chanel at her 1925 Paris collections, smart in black, toning in brown pigskin, and bright in orange suede. Fellow French designers Boulanger and Molyneux followed suit, providing a stream of sylish designer pochettes.

By 1926, not only the shape of handbags themselves had changed, but the very way in which they were carried was different. Even when bags still had straps, these were not always used, with large framed bags grasped by the top of their frame or tucked under the arm in the manner of the all-conquering pochette.

Black velvet and silver bag, c. 1920s, has a highly worked silver frame in Art Nouveau style. The velvet may not be original, as many valuable frames were reused, but this does not diminish its appeal to collectors and enthusiasts. The bag's clasp on its chain allows it to be suspended from a chatelaine belt.

The Arrival of the Coin Purse and Wallet

In the early years of the century, women of leisure had little need to carry money around. Goods and services were ordered, or paid for by others. But with growing independence and changing customs, it became desirable to carry a small bag in which to hold a little cash.

A tiny, 1920s lipstick-shaped "dance" reticule from France — made of celluloid, inset with paste and used for holding rouge, with lipstick hidden in the tassel.

The various functions of a contemporary handbag were often divided between several smaller receptacles. Women sometimes carried several small bags and a purse simultaneously; the purse was rarely hidden away in a handbag but was carried openly, either in the hand, on a chain around the neck, or hanging from the waist in the style of the earlier chatelaine.

Most purses were decorative, made out of silver, metal mesh, leather, fur, fabric, and many other materials, including more bizarre components such as a stuffed mink's head or an alligator's paw. Others took on the nature of jewelry. Solid metal coin purses of polished silver, gold, or gummetal came in all shapes and sizes, and often had separate compartments for different coins. They were sometimes attached to chains or long cords up to 50 inches (175cm) long, and were worn around the neck or across the shoulder, and

tucked into the belt. Some of the purses were so small that they could only hold a few coins.

Purse bags combined the functions of money-carrier and reticule bag and were used for formal occasions, while the increase in paper money led to the use of leather wallets by both men and women. Some wallets had additional pockets for coins, or were combined with card cases.

Silver mesh finger ring purses which hung from a short chain and a finger ring appeared in the early years of the century, and were used for dressy occasions. Other mesh and bead work purses resembled miniature framed handbags, with their twist knob openings, including chatelaine purses which hung from the belt or were pinned to the dress and worn indoors and out by both women and girls.

Satchel purses or purse bags made out of pressed, embossed German silver were exported in great quantities to the rest of Europe and

British finger purse (*left***)made from hallmarked silver with short chains attached to a finger ring. Engraved with the date, 29.9.09, and the initials G.J.**

America. Small and ornate, they were usually patterned with floral or Art Nouveau motifs, often with a small space left plain in the center for inscribing the owner's initials or a date. These purses were suspended on two short chains joined with a ring for carrying on the finger and were typically hinged at the base and fastened with twist knobs or a slide lock. They were lined with watered silk or leather, and held only a few coins at the most.

As leather handbag designs became more sophisticated, they were often made with a matching coin framed purse with the new twist knob fastening, a miniaturized version of the bag itself. Some were removable, others not, attached to the bag by a fine chain. In the 1930s, matching outfits were regarded as very smart, and this applied particularly to accessories. Hats, shoes, gloves, bags, and, of course, purses were all coordinated, as in Alexandrine of Paris's "Pif-Paf" design in *Vogue*, November 1935, of matching gauntlet glove, clutch bag, and purse in antelope hide, and trimmed with little leather chains.

Although many bags had a built in purse which opened with the revolutionary new zipper, the trend was halted by wartime restrictions on the use of metal. As designers and manufacturers explored other materials, metal zippers disappeared and metal frames were often replaced by wooden ones.

Wallets became fashionable, made as matching accessories to upscale handbags, and other new ideas were introduced, such as a slim black leather belt with pouch purse attached, sold by Harrods in 1948. These anticipated the frivolous attitude to fashion of the 1950s, which drew on earlier designs for new ideas, from chain mail coin purses slung from a plain curved bar pin and

a contemporary version of "grandmother's coin purse" made of gilt mesh by Fior in 1953. It was studded with rhinestones.

The first tiny patchwork fabric pocket purses for the body were launched by Jap in 1975, slung diagonally across the body on a long fine cord. This vogue for purses worn around the body was picked up by designers Clive Shilton, Bill Gibb, and Sonia Rykiel, whose waist-hung purses and wool hip-wrappers drew attention to the new languid lines of 1970s fashion.

In the 1980s, the credit card purse really took hold, starting with Chanel's 1985 gilt-chained, scarlet leather purse the size of a credit card. Gucci too produced a miniature purse with a gilt hand clasp of 1991, while Hermès's signature Kelly bag was miniaturized, to be worn on a strap

around the neck. Bags in miniature were made through the 1990s, including Chanel's quilted bags with tiny, matching purses, and those by British designer Katherine Hamnett.

By the mid 1990s, fashions had come full circle, looking back to the designs of the early 1900s with Anya Hindmarch's silver tassel purse and Erickson Beamon's evocative metal mesh purses and reticules, drawstring crochet tassel pouches and embroidered frame purses with jeweled chains.

The colorful needlework bag (*below***) features the Egyptian motifs fashionable in the 1920s. The frame is inset with colored, diamond-, round- and oval-shaped stones, with a chain strap and twist knob opening.**

Whiting & Davis

The popularity of the metal mesh bag as an accessory endured over two decades. One of the most prolific manufacturers was Whiting & Davis of Massachusetts, a company that weathered many of the social developments which affected the fashion industry during the early decades of the century.

There was a marked transition from handmade luxury items to the mass production of machine-made goods. At the same time, the role of women was changing. Not only were there now female workers in the fashion industry, but women were becoming active consumers for the first time.

Whiting & Davis began to make ring mesh bags in the late 19th century, the mesh formed from silver wire loops which were soldered together, initially by hand. Many of the bags were made by women homeworkers, reflecting, albeit on a smaller scale, the methods of other industries based on home labor, such as the Nottingham lace industry in 19th-century England.

But as early as 1910, Whiting & Davis had become mechanized and were producing high quality silver ring mesh to be fashioned into bags and purses. Many of these had ornate metal frames and jeweled clasps and some even had tiny clocks set into the silver frame. The bags were straight in shape or slightly flared at the base, and were often fringed, some with flap fastenings that were edged with silver and secured with a press stud.

The carrying chains were often just as elaborate as the bags themselves, and varied from fine ribbons to wide bands of silver. sSome of the mesh bags had tiny purses attached. The company made a range of purses, often with the fine mesh gathered at the base and finished with a tiny tassel. These measured as little as 2 x 4 inches (5 cm x 10 cm) and were held in the fingers, hung, chatelaine-style from the waist, worn around the neck, or twisted around the wrist on long, fine chains.

Whiting & Davis's production methods increased to meet a rapidly growing demand for their mesh bags, and they began to make bags in less expensive metals at more affordable prices. In the 1920s, flat mesh bags with patterns of an abstract, jazzy, geometric nature, in keeping with the

mood of the times, were produced. The patterns were formed by different colored links within the mesh, or by using different colored metals. Earlier examples tended to be made mostly of silver with odd bits of color, and were longer than they were wide, sometimes shaped at the base with rows of droplets. The later, larger bags were vibrant with oranges and reds, their frames also decorated in geometric Art Deco styles.

As a cheaper alternative to colored linked bags, Whiting & Davis also developed mesh bags which had a design printed onto them. They produced many of these in the late 1920s. Both flat and ring mesh were printed, the smooth, reflective surface of the flat mesh producing cleaner patterns than those on the ring mesh, which were less clearly defined.

The overprinting of the mesh meant that images did not have to be geometric, and could take on a more naturalistic, figurative quality. On the whole, however, most printed patterns mimicked the fashionable geometric patterns of the day.

At the peak of the mesh bag's popularity, Whiting & Davis dominated the American market. The leading French designer, Paul Poiret commissioned a mesh bag collection from Whiting & Davis towards the end of his glittering career, in the late 1920s. This became a virtual swansong for both designer and bagmaker. Whiting & Davis continued to manufacture metal bags until they finally went completely out of fashion in the 1930s. Today, the company has adapted its expertise to producing more unusual products, such as steel ring mesh gloves for use by butchers and chainmail suits of armor for costume dramas.

Mature Sophistication Takes Over

The movies of the 1930s offered a powerful escape from the economic depression and unemployment that followed the 1929 Wall Street Crash. First in America, and then worldwide, Hollywood movie stars such as Greta Garbo and Gloria Swanson became icons for a whole generation. It was fashionable to adopt a demeanor of languid sophistication, and make-up, plucked eyebrows, and nail polish were generally worn with longer, softer hairstyles. The romantic, flattering 1930s fashions contrasted with the gamine look of the 1920s, as women's fashions reflected a new maturity of outlook and skirts grew longer, worn mid-calf for day and full-length for evening. On more formal occasions, some dresses even had elegant trains. Handbags were still small, light, and glittery, but often less expensive than in previous decades. Economic restrictions imposed by world recession had led enterprising manufacturers to use new, cheaper materials such as Bakelite plastic to create similar sparkling effects. Bags with flaps like pockets or envelopes were the height of fashion, as were bags made from crocodile, alligator, antelope, and elephant hides.

Marlene Dietrich and her daughter (*left*) at a polo match in 1934, Hollywood. Dietrich's sporty ensemble is finished with a tiny beaded pochette, seen on the chair beside her. A typical 1930s rich red velvet evening bag (*right*) decorated with seeds and beads.

Special clothing for sporting activities became popular during the 1930s, and accessories to match were also required. Paper pattern companies provided patterns for this clothing, and for accessories, including hats, belts, and handbags.

SOBRIETY & AUSTERITY

Despite the glamour portrayed on the silver screen, clothes took on a new sobriety, at least for daywear, reflecting the austere mood in Europe and the United States. Clothes were expected to wear well, and to last for more than just a season, while accessories could update an outfit as well as effect a complete transformation. As a result, accessories became more dashing, used to relieve the stark economy and plainness of dress styles. By changing the hat, shoes, jewelry, and, of course, bag, the number of social occasions at which an outfit could be worn were greatly increased.

Hats took on all sorts of different shapes and styles. Many were jaunty, from close-fitting caps adorned with bows and paste brooches to wide brimmed felts and straws with striped grosgrain ribbon, all tilted at a rakish angle. Gloves were still essential wear, and shoes were heeled and substantial, while silk stockings made the new shorter-length skirts viable.

Belts with large buckles in marcasite, rhinestone, or plastic were an important accessory in the 1930s. Matching fabric belts, scarves, and bags were commonplace, some made at home from the envelope purse kits stamped on artweave that were advertised in magazines such as the *American Needlecraft Magazine* in 1930. The kits included a chart and directions, and everything to make the bag. Patterns for weaving your own belt and pochette were available in 1932, although commercially available coordinating sets were rather more sophisticated. In specialized New York stores such as Lilly Dache and Hattie Carnegie's pocketbook department, handbags could be ordered to match specific dresses or ensembles. Matching belts and bags were recommended for chic lunch party wear in 1936, and models such as the Virginia Art Bag were designed to be worn to informal occasions with "the Lady Carlisle shoe," both on display on New York's Fifth Avenue. In London, Asprey of Bond Street was marketing its striped black, gray, and white taffeta scarf and pochette.

The Pochette Continues

Many women still carried the flat pochette which had been so popular through the first quarter of the century. In the first half of the 1930s, all bags were carried close to the body, rather than swinging free, and both pochettes and framed bags with straps were held in the hand or under the arm.

Pochettes of both fabric and leather started the decade small and neat, but gradually became larger and more sculptured. Particularly desirable were reptile-skin flap-front bags with silver reinforced corners, made with and without finger straps. By 1934, the new finger loop handbag was being sold by Peter Jones of London, made of fine willow calf of navy, dark brown, or black. Finger loops were used on all types of bag, including fine examples

A French clutch bag, typical of the 1930s in its stylish simplicity. Made of black antelope suede faded to brown, and decorated with chrome geometric shapes, it has a deep flap front closing with snap fastenings.

of sequined evening bags hand-made in Belgium. There were reticules with petal-like flaps, while a sequined pouch attached to a gold-tone gatetop expansion frame went on sale in American stores such as Macy's. There were some frame bags around, however. Those with short handles for day and evening wear from the previous decade became sleek and discreet in the 1930s, and as in earlier decades, different occasions demanded different bags, with box calf bags for the least formal occasions and small, box-shaped pigskin bags to complement to classic tweeds. Frame bags made of gathered fabric, mainly in felt or tapestry, or in very soft leather or suede, were set into sculptural frames. The American company Koret, renowned for its beautifully made pocketbooks since the 1920s, continued to be a fashion leader with the clever styling of its handsome "Handbag Originals."

Afternoon Elegance

Afternoon clothes were often full length and very formal, and to accompany them, top-of-the-line afternoon bags were made by Cartier. Luxurious, costly, and beautiful, the bag's bracelet handle was made from tortoiseshell barred with gold, while the bag itself was made from satin-smooth black antelope and entirely lined with tortoiseshell-colored kid. The same year, 1935, designer Germaine Guerin introduced an elegant little bag that was smaller than average to lend it additional formality. The fine firm stitching hardly showed on the sooty background of antelope which threw the delicate gold mount into relief.

Jeweled monograms were also considered modish, found on models such as an afternoon bag of 1935 by the French designer Madeleine Vionnet in black antelope with a slender gold chain for a handle. Plainer models were enhanced by dramatic trimmings in the form of paste or marcasite clasps; on one Asprey pochette of 1936 in black antelope, the "platine" clasp was set with rhinestones.

A smart brown quilted calf 1930s clutch bag with a plain flap, was made in London by H. Wald & Co., a firm which produced high quality, well-designed bags and this one is no exception. The bag is piped in red and has a rust colored duchesse satin lining.

A typical 1930s six-sided creamy gold box bag (*below*) designed by Asprey featuring an ornate gold handle.

A high-quality brown crocodile 1930s day bag, probably made in England. Note that the skin variations have been cleverly used for decorative effect. This classic handbag is beautifully finished with a well-fitted cream kid interior, and brass frame and clasp.

A chic 1930s brown calf afternoon bag which has a chrome frame and faceted Bakelite handle. This handle is hinged so that it can lie flat and the bag is then carried by a discreet leather handle at the back.

As the leather and metalwork industries advanced technologically, bags were produced in a plethora of styles. For winter or formal daywear — to accompany tailored suits with fitted jackets and midcalf skirts that were made in jersey, corduroy, knits, and wool tweed — the 1930s trend was toward innovation in structure rather than decoration. Indeed, the detailing and decoration on bags generally came from their construction or were inherent in the skin itself, be it crocodile, snake, or ostrich.

Quilted jackets became fashionable, worn with a roomy bag in brown quilted suede designed for the country with a practical flap of calf; one was available from H. Wald & Co., London. By 1938, contrasting saddle stitching, tortoiseshell frames, and bookbinding effects were all widely used on bags.

Bags For All

In the 1930s, summer dresses with small printed floral patterns were worn by everyone, made in cotton, crepe, silk, and synthetic silk materials such as rayon, which was washable and cheap. Many of these designs were bought ready-to-wear, the fit of the garments adjusted by matching belts with plastic or paste buckles which accentuated the natural waistline.

Clothes were also increasingly fastened with metal zippers which, though still relatively heavy on light fabrics, allowed for the fashionable close fit. Zippers replaced both buttons, and hooks and eyes, and were even used as a design feature by Schiaparelli and other designers. Small, neat pochettes, carried high under the arm, were often made in matching dress fabrics, or in fine soft leather. Some of these, too, were zippered, one American example in black suede sporting a dog motif made of white fur, carried by a gold-tone metal ring.

Couture chic for rich New Yorkers

Macy's, New York's renowned Fifth Avenue department store, was a favored shopping place for wealthy, well-dressed American women. It provided high quality, long-lasting accessories that were definitely expensive, but those who could afford a "good" handbag regarded it as a wise investment — a philosophy which prevailed until the late 1950s.

These expensive bags were considered to be classic purchases, and the shelves of Macy's Little Shop for Accessories, positioned on the first-floor balcony, were lined with examples, including delectable pocketbooks by world famous French couture designers such as Madeleine Vionnet or Jean Patou. These handbags were beautifully finished, with surface details that reflected the tailoring and dressmaking techniques their creators were known for, including pintucks, quilting, and punched and stitched work. Movie star Greta Garbo (*right*) clutches just such a bag, a tiny pochette of snakeskin, as she sails for the Continent from New York.

With the natural look gone, completely superseded by the open acceptance of make-up, vanity bags were soon in ascendance. These, produced by increasingly successful cosmetic companies such as Elizabeth Arden, had existed for a while, but now began to be called beauty cases, becoming larger and more sophisticated. Upscale examples were fitted out with everything one could desire, and fashionable bags followed suit. One black suede afternoon bag from Selfridges of London had a mirror on the inside lid, and space for money and make-up. It was designed in 1935 to be carried at an "informal" evening dinner, despite the other encumbrances of fur cape, veiled hat, and long dress.

AFTER DARK

Sweeping trains and long chiffon stoles gave added elegance and emphasized the svelte lines of 1930s evening gowns, which were the perfect foil for bold jewelry: dangling earrings, long necklaces, and paste clips. Bare arms were adorned high up with slave bracelets, and wrists jangled with several heavy, jeweled bangles, or pearls wound around the wrist. Moiré pumps with high heels and an ermine wrap gave the finishing touch to the glamorous look.

Plain fabrics such as chiffon, silk, satin, silver and gold lamé, moiré, lace, and organdy were used for evening dresses, their only decoration the seamlines, pintucks, and fine pleats which traced the contours of the body. Long satin evening gowns cut on the bias were daringly figure-hugging and were often sleeveless, with low-cut backs or halter necks.

A 1930s evening clutch bag with a brocade fabric body sewn into a lizard-skin-effect Bakelite frame. The fabric is almost certainly not original — it would probably have been plainer and more stylish.

Lavish Decoration For Evening

Evening bags provided an ample opportunity for the lavish decoration which was absent from tastefully plain day bags. Beads, spangles, molded glass, and rich embroidery were all applied to small pochettes and frame bags set with inlaid stones. There was a vogue for texturing plain leathers and fabrics, seen on evening bags such as a 1935 small silver kid pochette, stamped in an ostrich feather pattern, or a 1936 bag of stitch satin with gilt frame and spring catch. In America, one black sequined bag attached to a gold-tone gatetop frame proclaimed its pedigree — a label inside reading "Hand Sewn Products, S.B. & Co" — while a gold kid evening bag on a jeweled frame and lined with satin was marked "Harry Rosenfeld Original." All the pocketbooks at another top New York store, Nat Lewis, were either one-of-a-kind designer originals or were actually created by store designers themselves.

On the other side of the Atlantic, Asprey of Bond Street, London, made brocade bags which fastened with a slide clasp mounted with rose quartz and blue agate. Their black velvet pochettes with a Persian plaque hand painted on ivory were also successful.

From the mid-1930s on, evening bags echoed the

A charming little 1930s beaded evening bag or purse, probably made in Belgium or France. The pattern of the beading echoes its pleasing oval shape. It has a purse style twist clasp and a small beaded finger strap.

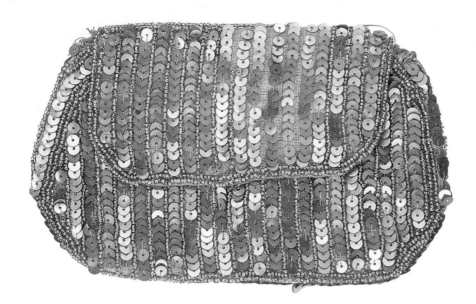

A 1930s clutch evening bag of sequins and beads on a canvas backing. The rich effect is simply achieved by vertical lines of gold sequins and glass beads. The front flap and the bag itself are edged with beads.

development of innovative shapes for day bags and also moved on from the small pochette or gilt chained frame bag. A musical novelty appeared in 1936, a velvet bag shaped like a banjo that was designed to be worn with vivid velvet gloves. An inside panel was pleated like an accordion, and the whole bag could be pulled flat if desired.

Bags From Top Designers

Following the first Surrealist exhibition in London in 1936, Surrealism took over from Art Deco in influencing fashion. The Italian designer, Elsa Schiaparelli, was at the forefront of this change, creating bizarre and daring objects out of unusual materials, such as a handbag in the shape of a birdcage, and one made out of transparent cellophane. French designers such as Molyneux produced themed outfits and accessories while Paquin, according to *Vogue* in July 1938, "girdles you with leaves and flowers; hangs a blossoming bag from your hands." On a royal note, across the English Channel in Britain, a gilt chained satchel commemorating Coronation Day in crimson velvet and ermine was on sale at Asprey's in 1937. Toward the end of the decade, the witty themed handbags of the top designers influenced the production of cheaper plastic bags, many decorated with appliquéd motifs on various themes such as an aquarium or a garden with glass flowers.

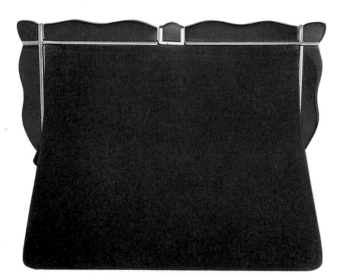

An elegant 1930s afternoon clutch bag made in black suede with a black Bakelite and gold-plated chrome frame. The gently waved edges of the frame and the intersecting lines of chrome make this bag a very chic accessory.

AT ONE'S LEISURE

All kinds of leisure activities continued to play a significant part in the social calendar. Casual wear and sportswear were specially designed for the lucky few who had not lost all their money in the Wall Street Crash of 1929, and the south of France attracted high society to the fashionable coastal resorts of Cannes and Nice, where a suntan became desirable. Trouser dresses, pajama suits, and beach outfits by Chanel, Hermes, and the like were worn with high-heeled sandals or espadrilles and, at the end of the 1930s, with platform soles. Leisure wear was often coordinated, as in the case of a 1931 navy and white striped jersey outfit by Heim, worn at Biarritz by Miss Europe. It consisted of full-length culottes, striped tank top, and matching flat shopper bag with short handles.

Bags to Accompany Beachwear

Linen and straw bags with appliqué or embroidered motifs were on sale from large stores such as the Galeries Lafayette in France — in 1936, it was selling a striped linen drawstring beach bag — as were bags made from new synthetics, such as rexine. In America, sparkling rodolac (promoted for its "shell-like surface that stays white!") could be cleaned with a damp cloth, and made useful bags for vacation or summer wear; cheaper varieties tended to turn yellow, however.

Spectator sports for the affluent required their own outfits and accessories. A woman's beige, patent leather race bag, lined with black, came complete with betting record book, purse, mirror, and notecase in 1932. Matching handbags and shoes became ultra-chic as coordinating sets came into their own, and in 1934, H. & M. Rayne, the acknowledged leaders in the field of coordinated outfits, advertised seasonal designs with names such as "Cleopatra." This line included matching bags and shoes available in black, brown, or white satin, studded with silver or gold.

Travel as an inspiration

By the 1930s, far more people traveled by car, train, and ocean liner than ever before. Adventurous designers experimented with boat shape bags made from various materials. The striking French leather pochette (*below*) was modeled on the ship, *Normandie*. It has three chrome funnels on top, the middle one forming the clasp. A silver chained anchor hangs from a porthole and there are four fine chain horizontal lines.

A young Katherine Hepburn (*right*) returns to Hollywood a star after her first movie appearance, a smart leather pochette clutched under her arm.

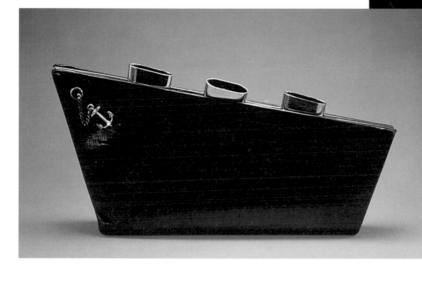

A 1930s French clutch bag is ingeniously made using a fake tapestry fabric specially woven to the required shape, in a charming traditional pattern of flowers and cornucopia, and edged in black. The weave is slightly metallic and the bag has a snap clasp.

Picking the right accessory

Accessorizing became increasingly significant through the 1930s, as women around the globe were urged to mix and match correctly if they wished to be stylish. Accessory charts began to appear in magazines, suggesting various combinations of matching or coordinating shoes, bag, belt, gloves, scarf, and jewelry to their readers in extraordinary detail. In 1934, for example, British readers were recommended to dress up woolen daywear with a plain leather, lined, gray felt bag from Fortnum and Mason, a wide double cummerbund belt in red felt from Jaeger, and soft gray cashmere knitted gloves and scarf from Debenham and Freebody.

By the mid-1930s, the variety of styles for accessories was so great that magazines could afford to be prescriptive: "For the small girl: wrong — clumsy bag, right — miniature satchel," wrote one. There was a general fascination with manners as well, and along with the magazine articles on the elusive qualities of chic, books on etiquette appeared.

Leather bags in all sorts of unusual shapes and unstructured styles began to appear alongside the more conventional large, pouched frame bag or the flat pochette. The latest designs in Paris in 1936 were a patent leather bag in a new tambourine shape, "cake box" bags, and soft pouffé-shaped bags with an egg-shaped frame. A triangular suede bag with shiny plastique frame and side lacing came from Model, who also made a round box bag of polished calf, with a round mirror hanging loose outside it in a suede cover. Stiff suitcase shapes with curved edges and corners bound in gold metal were made by Rochas, while in Britain in 1937, Asprey made a miniature portmanteau in black box calf, bordered with white saddle stitching. An advertisement the previous year proclaimed a new hat-box handbag in suede, with an oval quilted flat top as part of "the most exclusive collection of handbags in London." There was no recognized classic cut for bags, which were required to work harder than ever and were generally well gusseted at the sides or boxy in shape.

The Shoulder Strap Emerges

As the daytime silhouette became fuller toward the end of the decade, the way that bags were carried began to change once again. Straps were reintroduced on the big, pouchy bags of the day and were used to swing the bag once again, rather than grip it under the arm. The new fashion soon spread to evening bags, and by 1937, the triangular frame bag designed to be strung over the arm was all the rage. Gone at last

A purse-style bag from the 1930s made in soft, blue-grey velvet pleated into a V-shaped panel back and front. A twist-knob fastening in the embossed metal frame reveals a brocade-edged silk lining. Small rings show that there may have been a chain handle.

A witty bag made of black, faded to brown, antelope suede in a gathered knitting bag style fastened by a huge brass safety pin clasp. Possibly French, the bag is lined with cream duchesse satin and has a short suede handle.

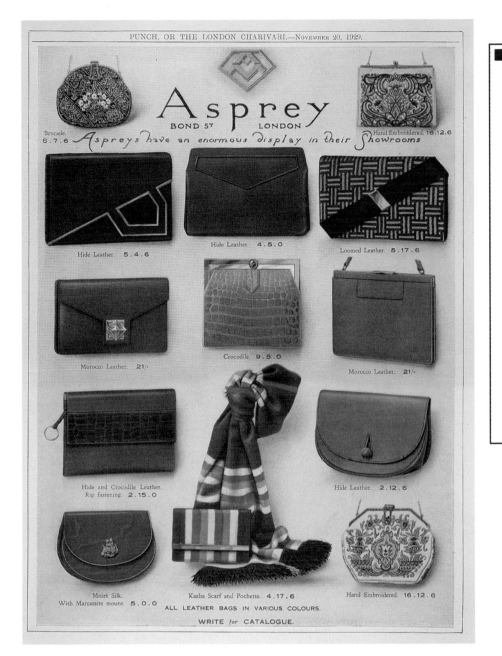

PUNCH, OR THE LONDON CHARIVARI.—November 20, 1929.

Asprey
BOND ST LONDON

Brocade. 8.7.6 — *Aspreys have an enormous display in their Showrooms* — Hand Embroidered. 16.12.6

Hide Leather. 5.4.6

Hide Leather. 4.5.0

Loomed Leather. 5.17.6

Morocco Leather. 21/-

Crocodile. 9.5.0

Morocco Leather. 21/-

Hide and Crocodile Leather. Rip fastening. 2.15.0

Hide Leather. 2.12.6

Moiré Silk. With Marcassite mount. 5.0.0

Kasha Scarf and Pochette. 4.17.6

Hand Embroidered. 16.12.6

ALL LEATHER BAGS IN VARIOUS COLOURS.

WRITE for CATALOGUE.

A advertisement for bags from Asprey of London during the 1930s, The range of colors and materials available to the fashion conscious woman of the period is evident, even from this simple illustration.

were the frantic attempts of chic socialites to clutch gloves in one hand, and bag and cocktail in the other.

As wide shoulders became fashionable and sleeves were emphasized, particularly in Schiaparelli's designs, bags continued to grow larger. The carrying straps grew longer, too, while skirts became shorter. By 1938 bags were more likely to be swung low on handles than to be tucked under the arm. The first real shoulder straps made their appearance with ensembles such as those of the American John-Fredericks, in 1939. The tartan-plaid cotton blouse and large straw hat with tartan-edged black veil had an accompanying shoulder bag to match, with buckled straps and top fastening. Large, sensible bags on long handles balanced the long jacket suits of the day, while pouchy bags on soft handles recalled the feminine styles of the turn of the century. But attractive as they were, the atmosphere was hardly that of the carefree 1900s, for World War II loomed and fashions were about to be put on hold once again.

Stylish bags at low cost

While the wealthy had no problem whatsoever finding stylish bags to match their numerous outfits, those with less to spend relied largely on mail order catalogs for their accessories. The cost of such bags was kept to a minimum by manufacturers, who employed synthetic and imitation materials for both bag linings and outers.

Imported wooden bead bags enjoyed a vogue, as did printed overarm bags with a tie bow top and headscarf to match. Washable removable slipcover bags in summery white linen were also popular, some with an optional monogram, and these were sold in quantity in the United States in 1938.

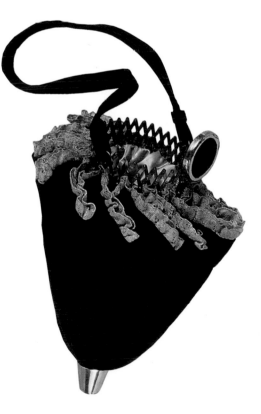

A 1930s mock parasol bag made of exceedingly soft black suede featuring a gold metal lid which operates like a concertina.

A beaded 1960s evening bag. Pink, luster-drop beads are sewn on to a sequin background and padded nylon body.

Evening Bag Fantasies

Ever since the handbag became an essential accessory, evening bags have provided the element of fantasy and indulgence missing from more functional day bags. Both decorative and personal, they encapsulate the glamor and elegance of high society.

Judith Leiber's first metal-based evening bag (*above*), chatelaine style, 1967.

Small, covetable, and costly, evening bags have appeared in every style and shape imaginable, and in the most luxurious materials, from velvets, embroidered silks, fine leathers, and bead and sequin work to silver mesh and molded cellulose. Many were set in ornate frames of silver and gold, tortoiseshell, amber, or carved ivory which reflected trends in jewelry, and were often adorned with real gemstones.

In the early years of the century, evening bags were fashioned from silver or vermeil (gold plating over sterling silver) mesh. The mesh was so fine that it felt like heavy liquid fabric in the hand, and was drawn together with silk cord or ribbon or set into ornate solid silver frames, which were often bejeweled. Some even had tiny clocks set into them.

During the 1920s, flat mesh bags with metal tassels and fringes featured woven or enameled geometric designs, their metal frames finished with Art Deco clasps and lift locks. Beaded evening bags were also favored, the best of which were handmade in France with the finest glass beads arranged in floral and scenic patterns. Their fringing and shiny reflective qualities echoed the beaded, flapper dance dresses of the time. The most expensive beaded bags were made with tiny beaded cultured pearls with pearl fringes from Cartier, whose evening bags were at the very top of the range.

Soft, elegant fabric bags made of velvet and silk inspired by the designs of Paul Poiret were carried from 1910 or so, some with petaled tops and long tassels. They hung from very long silk cords which were twisted round the wrist or finger, rather than worn over the shoulder. Brocade or embroidered bags in Viennese petit-point or Berlin woolwork also enjoyed a revival in the 1920s, each taking up to four months to make. Pochettes, decorated with dramatic Art Deco sunray or fan shape patterns, made in enameled metal, were also in vogue.

A range of celluloid vanities to contain lipstick and powder, some inset with rhinestones, were inspired by the newly invented plastics, dangling from tasseled silk cords. In the 1930s, plastics were also used to make entire evening bags, some with the striped designs that were considered so modern.

A Token of cCharm

Minaudières (combined compacts and purses) were first made by the French firm of Van Cleef & Arpels for Asprey of London, also in the 1930s. The name of the line was patented by Alfred Van Cleef as a tribute to his wife Estelle, who had a tendency to "*minauder*", meaning to simper or charm. They developed from small nécessaires, or vanity cases, the most precious of which were made by jewelry houses such as Cartier, Charlton, Tiffany, Ostertag, Boucheron, and Van Cleef & Arpels.

As government restrictions on materials took effect during World War, bags were often homemade.

A modern, geometric evening bag with accessories designed in the 1930s by Cloche Frères , France.

Many were simple pochettes of matching dress fabric enhanced by pins or clasps, while others were made by gathering a fabric suitable for evening functions onto a loop or ring.

Small, upscale fabric bags with ruched and draped satin were made by Paquin, and others with fringing and gold mesh with ribbon bows by Balenciaga. Fringing was a key decorative feature of 1940s evening bags, while black was smart in the 1950s. Black pochettes were rolled up like a jewel case and caught with a glittering pin, and black velvet chatelaines also came back into favor. Even more luxurious were evening bags of gold and white brocade, some embroidered with gold thread on velvet, others made of hand-painted satin or glittering with black, pink and gold opalescent sequins overlayed with sequinette lace through which the sequins shone.

With the arrival of the Swinging Sixties, curves and half circles were the new shapes, with evening bags in the latest plain, bright colors—especially pink and green—and shiny materials such as satin fabrics, patent leathers and "wet look" plastics. White plastic beading, silver and Perspex, and woven, gold and silver mesh were widely used, as were brocades in psychedelic patterns.

With the 1970s, formal evening wear became demure and ladylike again, worn with appliqué leather evening pochettes in pastel colors and bags shaped like shells, but by the mid 1980s, miniscule portable bags for parties were fashionable, especially in America, as well as revivals of earlier styles.

Earlier designs were picked up from the 1950s on, when Givenchy, for example, made mesh bags weighted down with jewel drops in 1956. Chanel favored box bags, making them from the early 1960s.

The tradition of minaudières which had been established by Van Cleef & Arpels in the 1930s was maintained through the 1990s by the American designer Judith Leiber. Leiber's minaudières and other evening bags, on sale in New York at the smart Saks of Fifth Avenue, are much coveted. Many of them are ingeniously designed to resemble a menagerie of whimsical animals, and encrusted in an allover pattern with literally thousands of colored Austrian crystals, each one painstakingly applied by hand. The American Anne Klein produced a range of elegant evening pochettes, while in Britain, Anya Hindmarch designed evening bags that were described as "tiny and fizzy as a fruit drop."

The large, pouch-like bag (*right*) was designed for the woman-about-town. It was made in the 1950s, possibly in New York.

Elsa Schiaparelli

Elsa Schiaparelli, one of the most influential designers of the century, was born in Italy but spent most of her working life in Paris. She was renowned for her witty clothes and accessories, precisely catching the theatrical mood of the 1930s in her own unique way.

Gold leather evening clutch bag (*above*) with dramatic black flap fastening, 1940s-50s.

Schiaparelli's work, despite its lightheartedness, was that of a perfectionist. Her bizarre imagery and revolutionary use of materials was influenced by the Surrealist painters, following their first London exhibition in 1936, and in fashion terms she was radical, challenging conventional color, form, and style. She took Paris by storm.

Although she pushed beyond the boundaries of convention in structure, decoration, and materials, she never sacrificed function or femininity either in her clothes or in her accessories, which proved to be the perfect vehicles for the distillation of her ingenious ideas. Her use of man-made materials such as waffled rubber, cellophane, plastics, and many others was revolutionary when she began working with them from the early 1930s, and the results were often beautiful.

She would transform a sober suit by the addition of an extraordinary hat or bag—her early collections, in 1935, included entirely transparent evening bags and belts made from cellophane and decorated with silver stars—and she borrowed designs and images from countless unexpected sources. There were bags shaped like flower pots and balloons, vanity cases made out of cork lifebuoys and a delightful 1937 light brown suede bag that looked like a snail.

The fishmarket in Copenhagen provided the inspiration for the first ever customized designer fabric. The old market women wore hats made out of newspaper, and in 1934, Schiaparelli put together a collage of newspaper articles about herself in various languages and asked the Parisian textile producer Colcombet to print the result onto silk and cotton. Colcombet sold length upon length of the customized fabric, which Schiaparelli had made into bags, blouses, scarves, hats, and a variety of bathing wear.

Her observations of manual workers who required sturdy leather ticket bags, from railroad staff to mailmen, resulted in 1936 in designer bags of rigid tortoiseshell for daytime use and mailbags of brown sheepskin and buckled buckskin. Purses in gold and silver lamé for evening wear, designed to hang around the neck, were modeled on the leather money pouches that tram and bus conductors wore.

The Introduction of Themes

Schiaparelli viewed each outfit as a whole, an outlook reflected in her range of themed collections. She recognized the talents of the artists and crafts people working with her,

and especially those of Jean Clement, an artist and chemistry graduate, and used them to create hugely imaginative bags. Clement contributed a number of original designs for handbags made out of molded, strikingly colored plastics.

In 1937, Schiaparelli's "Music" collection appeared, focusing on bags that played a tune when they were opened. In the "Pagan/Forest" collection of 1938, she made a football evening bag covered with black suede leaves, as always attracting plenty of publicity. Three weeks after the declaration of war, in October 1939, Schiaparelli produced

another show with the aim of liberating a woman's hands while retaining her femininity, in the form of huge pockets.

As she explored this idea further, knapsack pockets, stomach pockets like a hitched-up apron, and loose satin '"kangaroo" pockets all appeared, as well as a muff pocket on the front of a black crepe dinner suit.

In 1946, responding to new technology, she designed a coat for air travel with "suitcase" pockets. In the same year, an entire trousseau weighing less than 10 lbs (22 kg) including a reversible coat for day and night, six dresses and three hats, was designed to fit into her "Constellation" bag. Long, flap-fronted bags containing several compartments stacked vertically one on top of the other appeared in 1947, while the tongue-in-cheek 1949 bag with an umbrella handle was featured in French *Vogue* : "*Plus qu'un sac, moins qu'un parapluie*" ("More than a bag, less than an umbrella").

Schiaparelli continued to explore life without the handbag with designs that were pragmatic, aimed at working women like herself whose lives had changed for ever. For them, she devised her waistbags, fabric bags gathered onto a circular pair of handles to be carried over the wrist, and secret pockets in a 1951 dolman greatcoat, but the the tide was turning. Women's fashions in the decade to come would reflect a renewed passivity and constriction.

The famous bag (*left*), inspired by the newspaper hats worn by the women in Copenhagen fishmarket.

Fashion Feels the Pinch in the Forties

In a decade of cataclysmic upheaval, the end of World War II, 1945, was a momentous turning point. In fashion, there was a sharp divide in the styles of during and after, with the stark, austere costume of wartime abandoned as soon as possible in favor of the free-flowing, feminine fashions of the New Look. The practical shoulder bag ruled supreme during the war, but the elegant, impractical pochette soon regained its place in the affections of women eager for peace and domesticity when war ended. 62During World War II, clothing restrictions were introduced in both Britain and the United States. The first Utility Fashions went into production in Britain in 1943, following the issue of clothing coupons, and rule L-85 was introduced in the United States in the same year. Both restricted the use of materials which were necessary for the war effort, and for most people it was a time to tighten belts and make do and mend.

Women joined the forces (*left*) in unprecedented numbers during World War II, and the subsequent influence on fashion was far-reaching. Hexagonal evening box (*right*) brought chunky elegance to post-war Europe.

Luxurious evening bag made before the austerity of the war years (*above*), by Volupté, USA. A black grosgrain holder supports a silver-colored, gold trellis patterned box with jeweled clasp. Inside are fittings for make-up; a mirror opens to reveal compartments for cigarettes and lighter.

SHORT RATIONS

Women's magazines were full of handy tips, helpful ideas, and patterns for making everything from fabric shoes to knitted handbags. The availability of fabrics, and especially those of quality, was restricted, but women managed to improvize within the official limitations imposed, which even regulated the number of buttons that could be used. Unusual materials were exploited, including cork and wood for shoes, felt, blackout fabric, and parachute silk, and new kinds of trimmings were invented.

Paris, isolated early on from the rest of Europe as a result of German occupation, developed its own fashion trends and styles inspired by such star designers as those working for the House of Paquin and Jacques Fath. Paris couture collections continued to be staged throughout the war, although the Allied governments banned any publicity for them. In Britain, under the auspices of elegant designers such as Norman Hartnell and Victor Steibel, fashions remained static. The same was true in the U.S., although to a lesser extent, as homegrown talents were encouraged and designers such as Norman Norell and Claire McCardell came to the fore.

Tough Times

A shortage of raw materials and a lack of skilled labor in the accessory trades affected the manufacture of both shoes and handbags. At the beginning of the war, the United States had far greater stocks of materials such as leather and metal than Europe, where the shortages soon became acute. Shoes, the most hard-worked accessory of all, inevitably wore out and had to be replaced, in some cases reshod with wooden or cork soles. In Britain, the heavy, masculine Utility leather shoes were designed to last, with only brightly colored laces and contrast piping to cheer them up, but no frivolous straps or open toes.

Women were encouraged to polish their shoes properly, to guarantee their long life, and wore them with hand-knitted ankle socks in the winter, and bare legs in the summer. American silk stockings were the envy of all European women, banned in Britain at least, by the government.

Back to Basics

Commercially produced handbags became very expensive during the war, due to the short supply of metal necessary for the production of frames and clasps. Leather was also in short supply, although some luxury reptile skins briefly came onto the market as old supplies were used up. Zippers, too, were scarce, and handbag mirrors were banned, as glass was required for purposes essential to the war effort.

As a result, bags of all shapes and sizes were made at home, and easily made fabric bags in pochette or drawstring style were featured in magazines. One 1942 bag had

A beautifully constructed amber Bakelite box bag (*left*) from the late 1940s, has a hinged perspex lid topped by a large amber colored button ringed with paste, Bakelite, and brass.

A smart black crocodile day bag from the 1940s with a front flap closed by a rectangular gilt buckle. The overarm handle is attached to the bag by gilt studs. This is the ideal bag for the woman-about-town.

a rollover flap top, and was praised as being as "elegant as any that ever came out of a store."

Handbags were generally roomy and flat, with sturdy carrying handles and sensible, squared-off corners. The general opinion in 1943 was that big bags were best, allowing for self sufficiency. Most had short single or double handles. Those with a straight or envelope shape front flap fastened with a neat twist clasp or decorative motif, while top-fastening models were closed with strong metal clasps. Bags which opened with a zipper — popular before zippers became unavailable — often had two short handles and resembled sturdy shopping bags.

By 1944, clutch bags were large, elongated, and vast — the size of newspapers — while flat, chocolate-box shaped bags and round, summery bags with flat tops in washable fabrics were fashionable summer accessories.

Straight From the Shoulder

It was shoulder bags which ruled, however. These had begun to appear in the late 1930s, and became the bag style of the war years in both America and Europe. They were standard issue to the women's forces, but before long these military bags were mirrored in civvy street by fashionable satchel-style leather shoulder bags which fastened at the front with a buckle and came with adjustable, beltlike straps with side buckles. Other styles drew in at the top in flat accordion folds.

A dainty evening purse of the 1940s (*below*), the bag is hand beaded in a white herringbone pattern with gold beaded flowers on to a straight metal frame. The frame is engraved with a floral pattern, and the handle is a simple white beaded tubular shape.

Pockets for all

Early in the decade, handbags were sometimes replaced by large pockets and waist bags, similar to the modern fanny pack. These were largely inspired by Elsa Schiaparelli, whose original ideas for the outsize pocket came from her search for a substitute to the handbag that was functional and freed the hands. Her ideas were picked up in 1941 by the American designer Nettie Rosenstein, who designed a velvet almoner's waist pocket or purse, and Adrian. His lace-edged fabric patch pockets adorned summer dresses with such success that he opened his own salon in Beverley Hills in 1942 and won the Coty Award two years later.

Claire McCardell, another American designer, added a large patch pocket and attached an oven mitt to her housework-style popover dress of 1942.

A small 1940s evening clutch bag made of black velvet, gathered on to a curved metal frame inset with rectangular rhinestones, and opening with a lift clasp.

Gas masks had to be carried at all times — first issued to all members of the British population in 1939 because of the threat of gas warfare — and leather and fabric shoulder bags with long straps were specially made for this purpose, either by manufacturers or at home. While essentially practical, these bags in various colors could also be decorative, with some even matching party dresses.

The Shoulder Bag Evolves

The shoulder bag was available in a variety of styles, from elegant, slim versions to portmanteau-size sports models. One "wonderful great shoulder bag" with a knotted wide strap in red and white cotton-backed American cloth lined with gingham appeared in 1943, as did American Dick Whittington bags which were gathered at the top and had long straps. Country-style shoulder bags to wear with tweed and wool were usually made of leather and often trimmed with brass. One manufacturer of such bags was the British company Rowland Ward, whose hardwearing saddle leather country bags had horsebrass trim and a buckled strap. The American company Phelps handcrafted shoulder bags and wide belts with pouches in heavy calfskin, which were also decorated with antique brass trimmings such as harness bits, medals, and other militaria.

One year into the war, the impact of shortages was biting in Europe, and even in the U.S., top handbag designers such as Koret and Josef eventually came to embrace the new austerity, making the most of local supplies and techniques. Durability and functionality were essential wartime qualities, and strong, good looking bags were the order of the day. Although homemade bags often had to be made in softer

A versatile material

Felt, one of the earliest of all fabric materials and in production long before woven textiles, is made from compressed animal hair, wool, and fur. The resulting tangle of fibers provides a strong, often waterproof fabric that rarely disintegrates and holds its original shape well. As it was cheap to produce, felt was a natural wartime choice for making bags, especially since it was easy to handle and simple to decorate with stitchwork. So successful did it prove as a handbag material that a 1941 review of Paquin's brilliant blue felt bag and matching gloves with white topstitching and yellow lining reassured its readers that felt, in use since the Bronze Age, did have a future in fashion.

Tapestry bags such as this one on a gilt metal frame, have been popular for decades. Its clasp is decorated with marcasite and its handle is a delicate gilt chain.

materials, hardwearing goatskin and pigskin were favored for daytime use, with patent leather, kid, and crocodile the fashionable choice when available. To a great extent, sturdy fabrics such as tweed and grosgrain replaced leather — military equipment required quantities of leather — and felt was used extensively for both homemade and commercially produced bags.

Make Your Own

Women set to work with dexterity, making bags for themselves. In 1942, a rucksack in colored burlap to sling over the shoulder was highlighted in an article entitled "Accessories to make," while another stated that bags, "exempt from rationing but priced above rubies, will soon be every woman's desire. Here is a new use for cherished pieces of satin, scraps of heavy material, or fur fabric which must now be put into currency. Make bags to replenish your failing stock: give them as presents to your friends, who will be all gratitude."

By 1943, the big fabric bag was the fashion accessory to own, and all sorts of large drawstring bags to be slung over the shoulder were being stitched. Economical on leather, the homemade drawstring bag — in black suede or velvet lined with shocking pink satin, and featuring a broad carrying strap to fit over a glove — was often capacious and suitable for both day and evening wear. Commercially made examples, included those of black grosgrain or felt pulled up by drawstrings which were available from the London store Pissot and Pavy.

Envelope bags were particularly easy to make out of fabric and were useful for reviving a tired-looking wardrobe. Burlap, gingham, printed cotton, and bright striped webbing were favorites for summer. For once, the tables were turned, and bag manufacturers followed trends set by those making their own, imitating home-produced goods. One example, crocheted wool bags with tassels lined with cotton

An elegant black leather evening bag featuring an exquisite gold looped handle.

Probably a souvenir of the late 1940s, the bag (*below*) is made out of laminated postcards from Rio de Janeiro was a novel way to send greetings home. The postcards are carefully blanket stitched together in brown. The bag features a stone set metal clasp and is held by a wide brown silk ribbon.

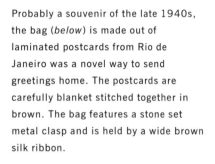

A black satin vanity case (*above*) with a large strap on top. It contains two separate compartments with a circular mirror in the lid. The development of the cosmetic industry generated a host of custom-built bags.

An unusual 1940s French evening pochette by Fior uses elements from historic embroidery styles on a modern material of the period, in this case, plastic.

During the war, women were employed as bellhops at the Hotel Astoria. Luggage styles remained static during this period, largely due to a shortage of raw materials.

print, could be bought over the counter at the London department store John Lewis.

Satin for Soirées

For evening bags, sparkling brocade and black felt were both admired in 1940, felt bags sometimes finished with a gilt clip, such as those available from Lafarge in Paris. Large grosgrain bags with a floppy bow at the top were sold in Galeries Lafayette, while in Britain in 1943, a vogue sprang up for collecting Victorian bead bags to use in place of a modern evening bag. These were conventionally carried by their handles or worn like a rich embroidered pocket, slung on a belt.

Most homemade evening bags followed the lines of daytime ones, although they were usually made from more exotic materials. Homemade satin pouch bags dangled from the wrist, while one very large triangular clutch bag of 1943 was made of stiffened satin bordered with lace. Other suggested styles to make at home included satin purses on long straps, and satin evening bags, jazzed up with a sparkling brooch or pin.

But as the war drew to a close, evening bags once again became the province of designers. The first sign of this in the United States was Mme Eta's Middle Ages Collection of 1945, which included a black rayon dinner dress with a sequined almoner's pouch at the waist.

The Matching Ensemble

Although fur ensembles of bags, hats, and gloves were readily available in the early 1940s, made by companies such as Mohlo of London in wallaby, Persian lamb, ocelot, or baby seal, they soon became harder to come by. Hat and bag-muffs were being made by Otto Lucas of New York, the muff four times the size of a tiny matching hat, and by Sally Victor, a leading New York milliner. Her 1943 mink hat and matching combination muff and bag was designed to be worn with a Hattie Carnegie red crepe ensemble.

When materials were scarce, color was often used to cheer up a neutral outfit. The brilliant green of a large crocodile bag with short handles, a green hat with red tassels, or a red hat and round red clutch handbag could make all the difference to a plain dress. Magazines advocated the making of bright-colored matching accessories right up to the end of the war, suggesting that they could add "the one and only color accent on a sober town outfit."

By the end of the 1940s, ensembles of matching bag and hat in a patterned fabric were worn in striking contrast to a plain suit. Designers such as Aage Thaarup created matching soft hats and soft bags in black-on-red bead

The red crocodile skin of this 1940s American day bag is treated almost like fabric to create a pouch shape with folds and piped seams. A thick wrist strap backed in red suede is attached to the back and the bag is finished with brass fittings.

This celebratory 1940s handbag in the shape of a champagne bucket, was, not surprisingly, made in France. Made of black suede with brass handle and hinged opening, the lid contains fake ice and the top of a champagne bottle.

Something old, something new

Despite the great popularity of the New Look, there were a number of protests and public demonstrations against the style, even in its birthplace, Paris. To the objectors, it appeared extravagant and élitist. The American designer Adrian was one who fought against the look, which he believed challenged both the hard-won patriotic achievements of American designers, and the development of American ready-to-wear. Most women loved it, though few of them could afford to suddenly change their entire wardrobes. Even the British royal family resorted to the ploy of most women rich or poor — they simply added lengths of fabric to their clothes. The New Look, far from making a quick exit, influenced every aspect of fashion thereafter.

embroidery, while a daytime ensemble of plaid sailor and plaid sac could be ordered from Pissot and Pavy. Not all bags were matching, however. By 1948, sophisticated soft drawstring styles of black satin piped in gold were available from Bembaron in London, and minute chatelaines made a comeback in 1949, made of black suede with pearl and gilt filigree clasps, or black velvet with petit-point medallion and silver clasp and chain. Pouch bags in tulle over pale blue satin twinkling with sequin sprays created by the American designer Nettie Rosenstein were also considered stylish.

THE NEW LOOK

By the time the war ended in 1945, women were more than ready for a new look. They found it in Christian Dior's collection of 1947, soon dubbed the New Look. In complete contrast to the masculine, pared-down economy of wartime fashions, the New Look was wide, long, and full, using up to 22 yards (20 metres) of fabric for the skirts of dresses alone. With nipped-in waist, voluminous skirts, high heels, and soft shoulders, the style was the apotheosis of the military look, and symbolized the transformation of the landgirl into the lady. Accessories altered completely to accommodate the New Look silhouette. Shoes were lighter and open, more feminine and frivolous. High-heeled, strappy evening sandals made of soft leather appeared, almost deliberately designed not to last too long.

Short, stylish haircuts replaced the long hair worn pinned up during the war, and berets and turbans were seen everywhere. With the New Look, hats became larger to balance the voluminous skirts, with wide brims, ribbons, and silk flowers, and were worn at a steep angle. By the end of decade, both these and smaller smart hats, which had made a comeback, were the height of fashion.

A 1940s summer clutch bag made in cotton in an abstract pattern of green, blue, and white triangles. It fastens with a geometrically shaped chrome clasp and has a pull tab. The fabric is reminiscent of furnishing fabric of the period.

An example (*above*) of the often surreal designs that emerged during the 1940s, this bag formed in brass resembles a birdcage, with lift-up hinged lid and metal base, with black cord straps. There is no identifying label and it has been suggested that it was a perfume container.

Postwar Paris

By the middle of the decade, French handbags were inventive and professionally manufactured, and were more sophisticated than those available in New York or London. Many French designers — Jean Dessès, Jaques Heim, Manguin, and Elsa Schiaparelli — sold handbags under their own labels from their ready-to-wear outlets. Hermes featured briefcase bags in box calf with metal locks, while Molyneux made ruched velvet muff-bags. By 1946, French *Vogue* featured evening boxes resembling jewel cases made by, among others, Madeleine Carpentier and Germaine Guerin. Very stylish leather bags by Morabito, Lucien Lelong, Suviane and Robert Piguet were designed to be handheld rather than shoulder length. Other, less conventional bags were of exaggerated length, with a long fastening strap looping through loops, and were shaped like an accordian or a glossy roll.

Many of these styles were inspired by the designs of Elsa Schiaparelli, following her return to Paris from America in 1945. By 1947 handbags became even more diminutive and featured complex fastenings and exterior pockets.

Handbags as Symbols of Hope

In Britain and the U.S., rationing was especially severe during the immediate postwar period. Bags were still not on coupons, and were often more expensive than the suits they accessorized. Nevertheless, British *Vogue* hailed 1947, the year of the New Look, with optimism and a plea for elegance. Handbags became smaller, but there was much more variety of style. Some were chunky and smart, whereas others showed a new softness. More casual drawstring gathered bags began to appear in soft leather or suede for use during the day, and fabric pouches for night.

Bags of crocodile, suede, antelope, patent, and even lizard-grained plastic for those on limited incomes (a good plastic was considered a better buy than poor leather) were available. Matching shoes and bag from British manufacturers such as H. Wald & Co. or Rayne were considered chic, although in 1949 it was even newer to have a bag made from green python, for example, and not to echo the shoes at all.

Capacious leather clutch bag (*left*) in brown leather is gathered in to cylindrical Bakelite handles, threaded through leather loops. The design makes bold use of the new plastic materials available to handbag makers.

An attaché style black leather case has a single handle and fastens with a briefcase style brass lock. Made in France by Prestige, the brass panel down the front is inscribed with various French holiday resorts, confirming this as a lady's traveling case of the smartest kind.

A striking brown antelope suede box bag with a mixed metal filigree frame, made in New York by Tyrolean NY. The padded lid has a mirror on the underside and the interior is lined in black taffeta. The bag stands on four metal studs.

Pochettes for Passive Women

Following the impact of the New Look, shoulder bags seemed unwelcome reminders of practicality and the war years. They suddenly became as unfashionable as short, narrow skirts and wide shoulders, and the pochette returned. Although pochettes still looked elegant held in the hand, they reflected the less active role that women reverted to once the war was over. Not surprisingly, this new feminine look was perceived by some as counterproductive to the advances that women had made during the war years.

A number of pochettes did have residual handles, however, including an elongated flap-fronted version in beige leather with a tiny handle made by Roger Model for Schiaparelli. And there were alternatives to the pochette, including fabric bags in unusual shapes. In 1949, one French model in twill by Pierre Balmain was gathered with two large bracelets, reminiscent of the 19th-century miser's purse, and the wide fabric strap of another, a round suede and satin bag by Albouy of Paris, was held by smaller wooden rings. Soft mulberry leather was used for handbags with pouched sides and a drawstring top, their spacious insides lined with silk. They were available from Lederer in London with matching purse, gloves, and belt. Hip bags came back into vogue, too, looking like large purses on a belt.

But the practicality of the shoulder bag made sure that it could not be ignored for long, and the shape was soon being employed to make functional travel bags. There were travel bags of other shapes, too, including one designed by Schiaparelli to hold a trousseau, and handbags shaped like half a hatbox, with a mirror as large as the lid, from the British designer Gay Kaye. Readers of a May 1949 fashion magazine were entreated to care for their looks when they traveled, and to make sure that their bag could carry toilet water or cologne to dab on brow, wrists, and hands as well as eyedrops to soothe travel-weary eyes. Cleansing milk, cotton, powder base, rouge, lipstick, and mascara were also considered crucial.

Bags for every occasion

Even at the end of the 1940s, it was necessary to have a handbag of a particular style for different occasions. To keep up with British social dress expectations of 1948, for example, the well-dressed woman was expected to carry a large leather drawstring bag for use at lunchtimes, and then a teatime bag that was small and slim, big enough to hold the merest essentials. A lizard handbag piped in sterling silver would have been typical.

By cocktail time, a woman's necessities would be moved into a bag that hung from the wrist, leaving her hands free to hold a glass and jeweled cigarette holder. Many such bags were made of faille and soft gold kid leather.

While she changed for dinner, into full evening dress, she would choose yet another bag; small and discreet, perhaps of snakeskin, or a little carry-all with filigree silver clasp and chain made of velvet or elegantly stitched in petit-point.

A funky American 1940s clutch made from multicolored wooden beads with a vertical beaded handle at the back. The bag closes with a zipper.

Stone-colored shoulder bag (*left*) in leather by Patrick Cox.

Long-handled tote, with side zip in naturally tanned "vintage 38 leather", handcrafted in U.S.

Shoulder Bag Practicalities

Shoulder bags liberated the hands, were capacious enough for the practical needs of the working woman, and made their stylistic debut in the 1930s.

The Dooney & Bourke "Arrowhead Essex" bag (*above*), made from all-weather leather, with solid brass hardware, is evocative of country sports,

The first shoulder bags to be noticed were designed by Elsa Schiaparelli in the late 1930s, but their functional, military look made them sure favorites in the war years. The shoulder bags of the 1940s reflected women's purposeful contribution to the war effort. They also liberated the hands, and were big enough to hold a gas mask.

A classic image of wartime France is of Parisiennes cycling from one part of the occupied city to another, with shoulder bags on their backs, but the idea caught on equally strongly in Britain and the U.S.

By the end of the war, however, women wanted a return to femininity and elegance. The shoulder bag was generally discarded in favor of short-handled bags carried over the crook of the elbow or in the hand. They maintained a position, though, in casual, summer, and country wear. Huge, flat, woven-raffia, sling bags with external pockets and matching belts were made by Walterna, while

British manufacturers such as Susan Handbags produced tan hide shoulder bags with adjustable straps and gleaming horse brasses for the country.

The shoulder bag was rejected less wholeheartedly by American women, perhaps because its wartime associations were less entrenched. American *Vogue* featured an ottoman leather shoulder bag in patent leather in 1951, to be worn with a narrow, Nettie Rosenstein city suit.

As the teenage market began to swell in the 1960s, the formal fashions of the 1950s were replaced by those appealing to a youth dominated market. Although handbag designers were temporarily at a loss, the casual shoulder bag was soon picked on as the style to fit the swinging new fashions, particularly the pants suit. Chanel's influential quilted bag on a chain strap, introduced in 1955, was widely imitated, and patent leather and plastic bags in bright colors filled the pages of fashion magazines. Top American designers created their own versions of the sling-strap bag, including Koret, Gretta, Wolfs, and Walter Katten, among others. They resembled conventional frame bags with a flap fronted or top fastening, but with longer straps.

Animated fashion shots of the time depicted long-legged models with flying shoulder bags on long thin straps by designers such as Mary Quant, whose shiny, black-and-white, PVC bags with long thin straps or chains were embellished with her ubiquitous daisy motif. Top designers such as Gucci followed with shoulder bags and "super-satchels".

By the late 60s and early 70s, ethnic influences were being adopted into mainstream fashion. Shoulder bags became large, and designers such as Adrien Mann and Thea Porter turned out embroidered bags, or models made from old carpets or patchwork. This development was mirrored in the U.S. with Gail van der Hoofe's embroidered bags for Allen Cole Boutique.

In complete contrast, tiny fabric shoulder purses on long thin straps were introduced by Jap at Joseph. They were worn diagonally across the shoulders, and sometimes worn in addition to a shoulder bag. Appliqué leather examples were created by British designer Nigel Lofthouse for Jean Muir.

The late 1970s saw a spate of soft leather bags with an integral shoulder strap, such as those made by Loewe. Pliable calf leather bags fastened with a zipper were first made by Enny and widely copied through to the early 80s. They had numerous pockets for the busy working girl, and were described in a 1978 advertisement in *Harpers & Queen* as "fashionable, yet soft and practical...plenty of pockets with zip and press stud fastenings for all those things you need to carry around with you."

As layered clothes became fashionable, so too did criss-cross straps for shoulder bags, several of which were often worn at a time.

A selection of contemporary shoulder bags from The Bridge, London (*above*) with matching accessories.

Satchels from Mulberry, and crossed canvas and brown leather bags from Gucci and Etienne Aigner were typical of the styles seen both in high fashion and on the street, and by the late 80s, shoulder bags had become a feature of everyday life for most women.

Prada's nylon shoulder bag with flap front, with a buckled and adjustable, nylon-webbing strap, set the trend for the liberation of the bag into the realm of the super-light, super-sport inspired culture. And alongside this fitness regime, the quantities of possessions that working women carry with them—from make-up to the laptop computer—made shoulder bags an essential accessory. Whether in the form of a shoulder tote of 1988, in chartreuse satin from Miss Maud of New York City, or Mulberry of Britain's country-inspired look, the shoulder bag now seems to be here to stay.

Classic DKNY style with broad straps and zip fastener, 1990s.

The Chanel "2.55", proves its enduring qualities by turning up in the Autumn/Winter 1997 Collection.

Chanel

Chanel is one of the most enduring names of haut couture, synonymous with simple-chic suits. But "Coco" Chanel's first love was millinery, a love which spilled over into an active and creative interest in all coordinating accessories.

Soft leather was handstitched (*above*) in diagonal parallel lines

Gabrielle "Coco" Chanel in the classic Chanel suit, with its braid-trimmed cardigan jacket, in 1966.

Gabrielle Chanel was born in 1883. She closed her couture house after the occupation of Paris during World War II, stating that "this was no time for fashion," but successfully relaunched her upscale designs in 1953, at the age of 70. Two years later, she designed her famous quilted handbag with gilt chain, which she named the "2.55" after its date of conception.

Chanel's clothes, like the 2.55, were functional but also highly stylized. She was well known for her inventive use of fabrics and skillful cutting, and had a particular talent for employing simple ideas, and seeing them through to their full potential. This resulted in classics such as the famous tweed suits with cardigan jackets of the 1950s and 60s. The cardigans had pockets which were designed to hold all the things that a woman might need in the absence of a handbag, such as make-up, cigarettes, and a cigarette lighter.

The pioneering, quilted 2.55 handbag was hand-stitched diagonally over padding to form a soft, quilted surface. The idea was said to have stemmed from Chanel's admiration for the quilted jackets worn by stable boys at the races. She already used quilting to line her jackets.

Variations on a theme

In 1955, the handbag was made in Chanel's favorite colors—navy, beige, black, and brown—either in soft leather (often lambskin) or her favorite fabric, jersey, and lined with red grosgrain or leather. The shoulder strap was leather, braided with flattened gilt chains, rather like those that hung on the inside hem of Chanel suit linings to weigh down the fabric. Since then, the quilted handbag and its variations have appeared in many different forms and colors, although the classic combination of black and gold remains the most popular. The linked "C" insignia on the gilt clasp—which also appears on her gilt suit buttons—is a more recent addition. Subtle variations on the original quilted bag emerged from season to season, in the shape or size of the bag, the gilt fastenings, and the strap. In a 1963 version, for example, the shoulder strap was threaded through large, gilt eyelets, and the bag was secured with a gilt twist fastening.

The monogrammed bag inextricably linked the design with the name Chanel. It was inevitable, given the high cost and classic status of the bag, that imitations would soon follow, but Chanel was shrewd enough to realize both the compliment and extra publicity that this gave her.

Chanel's Successor

Chanel died in 1971, and it was 1983, when the designer Karl Lagerfeld took over the boutique and accessories collections, before her name once again became highly fashionable.

His tribute to Chanel's trademark handbag varied from the respectful—his 1984 quilted black evening clutch was tastefully adorned with a rhinestone in each dimple—to less reverential later designs in the 1989 Collection, which were inspired by street fashion. They featured quilted versions of "B-boy" bum-bags.

In 1988, the House of Chanel produced eye make-up pressed into quilted blocks of satin-textured color in six shades which cleverly echoed those of the bags. In the same year, small white and red, boxy quilted bags on chains accompanied Lagerfeld's outfits, resembling power packs of energy. Versions of the bag continued to be made, such as the one in 1991 with a short shoulder chain.

In 1990-91, Lagerfeld designed a hat in the form of the classic quilted leather bag, complete with chain. It was worn high on the head and accompanied a pink and black wool, mini-skirted suit with quilted leather sleeves and monogrammed buttons. Evening versions of the bag made the same

year included a pastel blue, sequinned, flap-fronted quilted bag with a white leather and gilt chain. Lagerfeld's leather biker outfits of 1992-3 incorporated the classic quilted look as well as flap-fronted waist bags. Novelty versions have included tiny rucksacks, outsize traveling bags, and a hot water bottle!

A large shoulder sports bag in tan leather, oversewn with large white blanket stitching, was another Lagerfeld for Chanel design (in 1993-94), while his casual, beige leather drawstring bag had strings with

monogrammed gold bobbles, external flap pocket, logo, and matching loafers. A 1997 homage to 1950s plastic box bags was echoed in a clear plastic and gilt bag.

Each Chanel bag still involves 180 stages and 10 hours' of skilled work, but the company continues to fulfil all the criteria of a classic accessory, being functional, beautifully made, and instantly recognizable.

Coco Chanel was a pioneer of the total "look", and developed new lines of matching accessories, including jewelry, and the famous two-tone shoe.

Riding the Waves of Affluence

Once the immediate postwar period and the final years of rationing had been left behind, the stores were full of mass-produced goods and products and labor-saving devices and gadgets for the home-based woman. The washing machine became a standard appliance in the home, ideally matched to the new easy-care synthetics, and suddenly keeping up a clean and stylish appearance was no longer the struggle it had been before and during World War II. In the early 1950s, handbag styles, like other fashion items, did their best to distance themselves from wartime fashions. The newest bags were fine-lined double envelopes, designed to hold slim accessories rather than bulky ration books and other wartime paraphenalia. As metal and leather gradually became available and less expensive, the handbag, a very costly accessory at one time, again fell into a cheaper price range that most women could afford.

Princess Grace of Monaco and her daughter, Caroline arrive in Paris for an official visit in 1959. Mother and daughter clutch Kelly bags, made famous by Grace before her marriage. A typical 1950s bag (*right*) made out of Bakelite and featuring a metal clasp.

Striking Miami Beach-style
1950s bag (*above*).
Beautifully proportioned, it
has a gold-colored frame
over a black velvet body.
Hinged lid and rigid handle
are black plastic and the
fittings are brass.

THE NEW LOOK GOES ON

Despite the formality of 1950s dress, outfits became more multifunctional, and day suits, with the removal of the jacket, revealed lowcut tops for after-work events and cocktails. Younger women led social lives that were less rigid than those of their elders, and American designers, particularly, created clothes and accessories with a less socially static and conservative lifestyle in mind. In Europe and America, the stiffened, full-skirted New Look continued to excite women and designers alike, particularly for evening wear, and a narrower silhouette also developed. Jacques Fath designed a line of high-waisted dresses in 1953, leading the way toward the high waist fashions seen everywhere by 1958, accompanied by shorter, rising, widening hemlines that anticipated the dress styles of the 1960s.

As fashion photography developed into an art, models in fashion magazines and advertisements posed in static positions with gesturing hands and immaculately made-up faces. They were still modeling specialized clothes for different occasions, as well as less formal clothes for home-based activities. Of these, the "little black dress" for cocktails proved the most enduring.

Lady-like formality was the order of the day, and outfits were never without the prescribed accessories for the occasion. Close-fitting or cartwheel-shaped hats were widely worn, while shoes were higher heeled than they had ever been before. Gloves were still essential for day and evening wear.

Never Without a Bag

After the recent economies of war, women enjoyed their accessories and would often buy complete ensembles at a time. Stores such as Hattie Carnegie's in New York were able to dress women "from hat to hem," as her advertisements proclaimed, although some bag accessories could be a bit eccentric. One novelty of 1955 was a blue plastic and chromium hook from which handbags could be suspended from a table.

Matching accessories were also very fashionable and included both matching colors and fabrics. The working rule was to match shoes and bag in color and texture, although it was thought best to keep gloves a different color from the bag to set each other off better. Needless to say, the rule was dramatically broken on occasion.

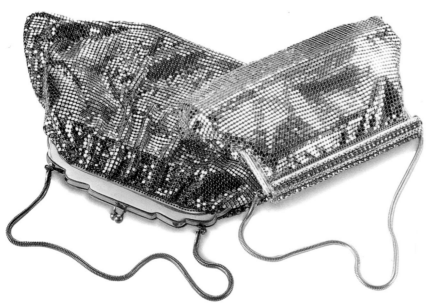

Two evening bags (*left*) from the late 1950s
made from chain mail of tiny hexagonal discs
over a lining. One is silver, the other gold and
both have thick, close-linked, cord-like chain
handles.

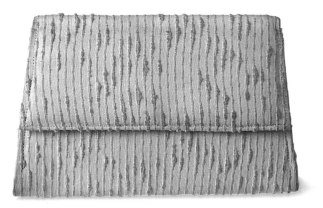

A 1950s clutch day bag (*above*) made in cream slub silk. A simple, elegant bag whose only ornamentation is provided by the rough texture of the fabric; its flap is made to exactly match the bag's body shape.

Amusing newsprint-fabric 1950s day bag (*left*), possibly from the U.S., it is decorated with a fabric horse and rider picture, a red ribbon rosette and rhinestone motifs. The bag is laminated and has a cheap plastic lining.

Magazine features on color schemes advised on how matching gloves, bags, and cravats could be made out of dress fabrics at home, while large stores such as Hattie Carnegie's had custom-made pocketbook departments where handbags could be ordered to match specific outfits.

Taking the Lead in Design

Many top designers recognized the profits to be made in ready-to-wear clothes and accessories, and sold accessory designs under the umbrella of their design houses. Sales were increasingly international, which led to the work of British designer Jane Shilton being featured in American *Vogue*, for example, and Mark Cross was profiled on both sides of the Atlantic. Waldybags, Fior, and Finnigans were names familiar in Britain, while in France, Roger Model designed some wonderful bags for Hubert de Givenchy and Jacques Fath; Kirby Beard and Francis Winter were also well known designers of the period.

The major Italian bag designers were seen everywhere, as boutiques and "stores within stores" began to proliferate. Italian handbags from design houses like Gucci were imported in huge quantities by the British retailer Susan Handbags, of New Bond Street, London, and by Macy's Little Shop for Accessories, in New York, although large American stores had plenty of leading native bag designers to choose from, too. Of these, Josef, MM, Hattie Carnegie, and Walter Katten were among the most highly sought.

Making the Most of Materials

The unbeatable qualities of leather guaranteed that it remained a leading choice for bag manufacturers, who had an ever-widening variety of skins to choose from. Velvety soft antelope, smooth calf, textured ostrich skin, softest gazelle from Italy, pigskin, and hide for the country, often with saddle stitching, and the expensive

Fastenings with style

The quality of a handbag was evident not only in the leathers used but in its fastenings, which developed new sophistication in the 1950s. Fastenings such as slide locks, twist locks, and briefcase locks were appreciated for their strength and practicality, but were also used as a decorative feature in their own right, especially on plainer day bags. No-clasp bags such as the small, half-moon pochette shapes of 1954, sold by Bagcraft, opened with the ingenious new method of pressing the frame at the sides, while a 1954 business bag from Ronay of New York was promoted for its new spring silent closing.

A stylish basket bag (*below*) for evening made in the U.S. by NYC Llewellyn Inc., of black molded perspex, and boldly decorated with large, symmetrically placed rhinestones.

reptile skins were all easily available. From the mid-1950s on, reversed calf and smart patent were the leathers of choice. Formal fabric bags were generally trimmed with leather, while the new synthetic fabrics were practical for functional accessories. Cotton, taffeta, and mohair were all widely used, often combined with plain or decorative leathers, and in the early 1950s, cheerful drum-shaped shoulder bags in plaid taffeta and leather were fashionable. Mohair was used on satchel styles from companies such as Bembaron, backed and flapped in cherry red calf, and mohair pochettes enjoyed a vogue in 1952.

Novelty yarns such as tweed leather were appreciated for their contrasting textures, although overall, fabric handbags assumed a new look by the end of the decade, taking on a softer, pouched shape. Many were made of corded wool, knitted and ribbed with calf trimmings.

Reptile Skin Classics

Reptile skin handbags, popular for most of the century, were the cornerstones of a woman's wardrobe in the 1950s. They were considered an investment which would stand a woman in good stead for many a year, and were expected to age gracefully. Upscale companies such as Mappin and Webb of London had countless overseas outlets in cities from Paris to Bombay, where their goods, from jewel cases to crocodile and leather handbags, were sold.

The most expensive of these, including alligator bags by Cartier, crocodile bags by Jane Brak of Paris, and cedar crocodile handbags by

Zany plastic bags with lasting appeal

Plastic handbags, mostly produced in New York, first became popular toward the end of the 1940s as postwar fashion designers embraced modern technology. Bakelite and cellulose handbags and vanity cases had been fashionable in the 1920s and 1930s, but it was not until the 1950s that the full, if shortlived, potential for rigid plastic bags was realized.

Many early plastic handbags were molded into simple, transparent box or round shapes, but as those working with plastics became more skilful, ornate bags of extraordinary complexity were produced, despite their downmarket destinations. Some were unique while others mimicked traditional handbag styles, patterned to resemble skin or brocade. As the quality of plastics improved, they were used more and more for cheaper, younger styles, but also to imitate natural hides. One, an imitation pigskin called Pigadex, was available from Universal Leather Goods in 1954, while

Ecalon, another practical hard-wearing leather substitute, was recommended for younger fashions the following year, as was imitation ostrich. Early plastic handbags were expensive, but their prices dropped dramatically as more were made. Eventually the market collapsed in an excess of kitsch, but today, extraordinary plastic handbags made by companies such as W. J. Roeder and Co, Ltd. are avidly sought by collectors. The case (*below*) by Gene, has a two-dimensional tableau on the front made of cardboard cutouts, covered in clear perspex, with handle and fittings of brass.

Actress Sophia Loren walks hand-in-hand with her husband Carlo Ponti outside Penn Station, New York. Her handbag is a large, Gladstone shape with top and side fastenings.

A spider's web in beadwork against black velvet makes a dramatic decoration for this US-made day bag.

Asprey with matching shoes by Rayne, were unmistakeable status symbols. A crocodile handbag in brown or black was one of the most desired and expensive of all; a magnificent black crocodile bag made by the English company Waldybag, cost £52 (a huge sum at the time), but was finely lined in suede and was made to last.

Early in the decade, Americans took a fancy to black and white. White alligator was the spring successor to the black alligator bag lined in red capeskin from Nettie Rosenstein, and in 1952, gray alligator made an appearance in a bag by Koret, from Bergdorf Goodman. It had an outside pocket and the inside was fitted with a secret compartment. Nettie Rosenstein also designed pewter lizard skin pumps and delicately framed alligator bags with short handles, which had a matching twist snap purse and mirror. These looked good with stylish day suits, dressed up by three rows of pearls and a neat hat.

A late-50s evening clutch bag by Eastern Arts Corp. New Delhi, India. Floral and geometric motifs embroidered in silver make a bold statement against a black velvet background.

A Healthy Diversity

As in previous decades, dressy pochettes led the way for evening wear, while daytime bags generally followed classic structured styles. There were chic bags for cocktails, sturdy shoulder bags for the country, and basketwork and cotton bags for summer vacations. Some small tailored bags picked up on popular trends outside the fashion world, such as the 1950 music-roll bag by the American Koret. There were boxy shapes, such as a tulip shape bag by Fior of 1951, binocular-shaped shoulder bags, and bandbox shapes, some with rounded corners and rounded silhouettes.

Most day bags, however, were suddenly very large and capacious, including the many purposeful styles of mass-produced bags. Tough but neat calf bags were available from the British chain store Russell & Bromley in 1950, and square, roomy, calf handbags with an easy-going rolled handle came from Finnigans.

In 1953, handbags had a new tailored dash, some tiny as a man's wallet, others as big as a briefcase. A brief fashion for doll's size handbags sprung up when the French designer Roger Model for Hubert de Givenchy featured them in the collections of that year. The black crocodile leather was fashioned into miniature bags in purse

An evening clutch bag with an asymmetrical flap edged in gold, and bold embroidered design which follows the shape of the flap. There is a side tab with which to hold the bag. Cornucopia, London.

Charming amber Bakelite beehive bag (*right*) made in the U.S. in 1951 by NYC Llewellyn Inc. The top is cream colored, suggesting honeycomb, and is inset with three small brass bees.

This 1950s bag (*above*) exemplifies the *Vogue* principle "better a good plastic than a poor leather." Made in the United States by Wilardy in white pearlized plastic, it is simple and elegant.

A day bag (*below*) by well-known English maker, Rayne, of dull gold metallic fabric, gold leather side gussets, top, and double handle.

and boxy shapes. In the same year, large overarm framed bags in shiny or matte leather with zippered or twist ball tops were also fashionable, some with an accordian shape at the base. Business case-like shapes were huge and heavy with briefcase fastenings, and some were even brass studded for extra durability and styling on their wide bases.

INFORMALITY REIGNS

From 1954 there was a fashion for bags with bamboo hoop handles, both squared or rounded. It started a trend for distinctive handles that led to a vogue for mock tortoiseshell handles (and buttons), and then soft, swathed handles in 1955. Metal ring handles were featured on a tweed bag that was especially designed to wear with what was advertised as "America's best loved suit," a tweed suit from Handmacher.

Decorative handles became a feature of both upscale and everyday bags, and in 1956, Roger Model for Hubert de Givenchy featured a white handbag with crocodile handle and flap detail. Another, in white leather, had a squared bamboo handle with a metal sun fastening. More prosaic pouched nappa leather bags were carried by soft twisted or plaited handles from 1956 on, while handles were even made from iris roots in 1957, in the manner of earlier bamboo and birch bark handles. Earlier, though, handbags had begun to develop wide handles, and wide bases. Some turned into the dumpy, smaller, soft feminine handbag in deep "grandma" style, while others were long, narrow, and capacious, often with double loop handles and simple knob fastenings. With their leather soft and rounded, these bags had no hard corners, and their built-in handles and sturdy American-style tote handles made them practical and hard-wearing.

The fashionably curvaceous lines of bags meant that even envelope styles were padded and not stiffened. Pochettes, too, had plumply curved shapes and new clear lines, including half saucer shapes and a pouched 1920s look on wide curved frames.

The new softness of 1955 applied to crocodile bags, too, which became as supple and pouchy as suede.

Creating Contrast with Color

Just as clothes were emboldened with accessories, color began to brighten leather both on day and night bags. Aniline dyeing techniques used to color leather were improving all the time, and in 1954, shocking pink, to wear with white, a murky yellow and a subtle willow green were achieved for the first time, and soon became fashionable. They were made up into bags and shoes, with gloves and tall umbrellas to match.

From the mid-1950s, colors really began to sing. Bags were used to balance and reinforce the color scheme of an outfit by adding contrasting line, texture, and color. The summer galaxy of new fashion colors included sage green, garnet red, Wedgwood blue, maize yellow, and sugar pink, as well as marigold, lilac, red, and sapphire blue. Winter colors were the more muted tobacco browns, beaver brown, and cafe-au-lait.

The American taste leaned towards red and black bags with thick gilded settings in felt, suede, and grainy leathers. Bright red satchel bags with a red felt stripe on black calf were typical of the trend, made by Roger Van S, from Bergdorf Goodman. There was also a craze in America for patterned, striped, printed, or stitched bags. Red and white leather carryalls stitched into sizzling stripes were designed by Josef at Bergdorf Goodman, who also created barrel bags in striped black and white leather that looked like awning canvas. Printed plaid small leather envelopes in Loewenstein calf were made by Jana, while polka dots printed on black patent leather were made into striking bags by Mademoiselle, Colonial, and Lennox in Loewenstein leather. All were worn with spotted shoes and gloves.

In Britain, a new prettiness in leather came to the fore, with pink and green rosebud prints on a slim pochette and matching shoes from Rayne. Flower printed clutch bags with snap tops in printed Ascher silk and Liberty print cottons appeared in many stores in 1956.

Farewell to the Daytime Pochette

Pochettes were generally large and sleek in the 1950s, and started to become elongated early in the decade. Some were rolled up like a jewel case and caught with a glittering pin; others had a flap front, straight or curved, which echoed the curved waisted jackets of the handsome 1950s suit.

An Italian bag from the late 1950s in black plastic made to look like straw. The brass handle is molded to look like bamboo, and the frame is etched with a bamboo motif.

The appeal of fur

In the late 1950s, a sudden craze for fur bags hit the fashion industry. It wasn't a new idea — Jacques Fath's gray flannel suit of 1954 was featured with pointed cap, cravat, and wide, curly Persian lamb bag — but was taken up in earnest in 1957, unencumbered by more contemporary qualms about working with fur. The new fur bags were designed to be worn as the only accent with plain suits, and definitely without matching hats or stoles. In Britain, Jane Shilton designed huge flat bags of cheetah fur with brown calf flap and handle, and oval-shaped bags and purses in fluffy gray American opossum, with black calf frames. She also made fur purses in velvety black moleskin and fur belts in brown and white baby calf.

Bembaron at Fortnum and Mason, in London, sold portmanteau-sized bags in subtly shaded sleek fur, with black calf frames and handles, and Parisian bag designer Roger Model made bags in panther for Givenchy. Almost square, dappled ponyskin bags in black and white were made by MM from Lord and Taylor in 1955, while large frame bags of leather with panther sides and ponyskin bags by Walter Katten were featured in the August 1958 edition of *Vogue*.

From vacations to high fashion

Although practical drawstrings were often used as vacation bags, baskets soon came to epitomize the vacation spirit. Cheap and cheerful baskets were made from woven rushes, while more sophisticated raffia baskets, and black laquered straw trunks complete with a gilt lock and key were made by the Eaton Bag Company in the early 1950s.

This was not just a fashion of economy, however. In southern France, rather more stylish straw bags were carried, and in 1956 a polished shrimp basket fitted with compass was available from Elizabeth Arden. A 1957 fad for casual straw baskets with cloth lids underlined the fashionable cachet that baskets now had, and by 1958 huge, hand-made baskets were featured in many fashion shots in upscale magazines.

Early in the decade, a downscale fad for "glamour baskets" was started by Dorset Rex of New York. Such bags were never alluded to in high fashion magazines, but were wellknown to the "dance hall" crowd.

The cheerful cherry summer basket bag (*below*) was made by Las Doradas in the United States in the early 1950s.

Clutch bag and matching zipped purse from the late 1950s made of gold, glitter-effect plastic. The bag has a snap clasp and a mirror pocket on the inside back wall.

Black calf envelopes were considered stylish, most very long, flat, and narrow. Some were piped with sterling silver beading, although many others remained plain. Some versions, a cross between the pochette and the handbag, featured a flat hand strap at the top, through which the fingers slid. One from 1955 was a large, flat, red coral calf pochette with a top handle from Bally of Switzerland. The variety of design was enormous, some folded with a sprung gilt handle, others closed with a briefcase fastening. But despite their originality, including a new bean shape, pochettes set the wrong tone for daytime use, and by 1958 were reserved for evening wear only.

Rise of the Casual Bag

Increasingly large numbers of women needed stylish but casual large bags, but did not want to carry a handbag as well. As a result, shopping and casual bags began to play an important part in the wardrobes of working women in particular, who needed to take cosmetics and accessories to the office to dress up for an early evening date. Casual bags — categorized as such by their use of more flexible leathers and tough cloth — appeared in all shapes and sizes, from raffia and straw baskets for casual days, to neat waterproof carryalls that folded into small envelope shapes when empty. Baskets and bucket bags, a new style from France, were lined to match showerproof coats. Bucket bags were

Molded plastic box bag with inset artificial flowers and fruits made in the U.S. in the 1950s. The handle is also plastic. Bags like this became very popular and now have become highly desirable collectors' items.

typical of the 1950s, reaching the height of their popularity in the middle of the decade. They were cheap to buy — as long as they remained open-topped they were exempt from purchase tax — and enormously useful and capacious, managing to be a fashionable accessory despite being able to hold several pounds of vegetables. The fact that they were open topped meant that linings were a feature, although only tough fabrics looked right; others remained unlined. They were practical, usually made in substantial leathers such as hide, but rigidly inflexible and a nuisance to carry. Nonetheless, they accompanied all sorts of incongruous outfits, from dresses to smartly tailored suits, leading to gentle mockery in cartoons.

A lighthearted 1950s summer basket bag, probably Italian; white painted wooden beads form the body and handle, and base and lid are straw.

This pretty shell-shaped evening clutch bag of the late 1950s, has a scalloped edge. Shiny white beads give it a silvery appearance and larger beads pick out the ribs of the shell.

The Useful Drawstring

Less rigid, more informal casual bags included those made in soft fabric, such as a knitted green plaid bag of 1951 with tan leather handles. Drawstring hide bags were typical of 1953, some in a sherry color with leather tabs on a cord, others made of canvas, and leather shoulder saddlebags, such as those sold by Liberty's, on London's Regent Street. High-quality nappa bags, as soft and pliable as a glove, were sold in Harrods, their thong handles looped through golden rings. Soft sack bags by Fior were made of black antelope, and large, soft, pouch shapes with zipper closings and double handles often had matching calf notecases and compacts. Upscale totes and shoppers in coach hide, often in tan, came with simple soft edges, a double loop handle, and gilt ring mounts. The most glamorous examples were made in black patent leather, with tote handles; one 1954 example featured a side purse with separate frame and lined with moire.

Evening Bags for Romance

As an increasingly stable economy encouraged a return to formality for after-dark occasions, strapless ball gowns with full tulle skirts reached the height of romantic femininity in the 1950s. They were made in the U.S. by designers such as Ceil Chapman and Charles James, and in Europe by Jean Dessès, Norman Hartnell, and Christian Dior, and were complemented by exquisite evening bags.

These minute shells often held little more than the flimsiest of handkerchiefs and the smallest of combs, and were made from expensive petit-point or gold and silver kid leather. Kenneth Rouse designed his velvet chatelaines tasseled in silver in 1950, and matching evening accessories in fabrics such as brocade and metal lace appeared in the same year.

Diamanté bags were regularly worn with ballgowns, almost as an additional jewel. Such bags would have caught the light from every angle, especially when carried by hands gloved in rhinestone-studded black suede. Many of the original quality designs were stunning — some were frosted all over with rhinestones, such as a

This evening bag was hand-made exclusively for Le Soir Handbags in the late 1950s. The body is covered in gold sequins, to each of which is sown a conical yellow plastic bead threaded with tiny yellow beads which also decorate

A novelty poodle bag made by Walborg of Belgium. The dog is embroidered with black beads.

A transparent box bag of etched perspex. The rigid form is complemented by soft black velvet cord handles.

White plastic vanity case made by JR Florida, with a perspex handle. The decoration was probably applied after purchase.

Woven raffia basket made in Japan for Ritter. The lid is decorated with velvet strawberries with green ribbon leaves.

A U.S. made evening basket bag of black molded perspex decorated with large rhinestones.

A typical 1950s evening bag giving a mock pearl finish with a circular gold clasp and gold decorative features on each side.

A soft bag of snakeskin with an elegant Bakelite handle and fold-over lock.

A Japanese summer straw bag, decorated with a raffia poodle and colored beads, and laminated in clear plastic.

A cross between a vanity and an evening bag, this plastic bag holds very little beyond cosmetics and change.

Two beaded evening bags: the gold bag is decorated with two types of gold beads sewn with gold thread; the other bag is decorated with purple sequins and purple-lustered pearls.

white satin handbag with slender chain of 1952, from Galeries Lafayette — and were quite sturdy, supported on a strong frame, despite looking fragile.

There were rounded shapes such as a matching large ball clasp purse and gloves in antelope studded with rhinestones from Gants Aris of Paris in 1952, and practical pouched shapes with wide wrist straps completely covered with sequins. Opalescent sequins were often used, sewn into geometric patterns. On one, black and pink sequins were worked into a checked pattern, and set on a gilt frame covered with paste stones and with a gilt filigree clasp. Slim black velvet and rhinestone pochettes made by Fior in the early 1950s soon became classics, as did satin bags on a curved frame with a handle by Lafarge. Indeed, by 1953 black was a steady "must" for theater, cocktails, formal luncheons, and informal dinner parties. As cocktail gowns and bouffant evening dresses became more and more extravagant, so formal, black evening bags became a standard night accessory, the black background often enlivened with shimmering sequin colors.

Dressing for Cocktails

On the whole, cocktail and afternoon bags were slightly less formal than those used in the evening. A typical cocktail outfit of 1952 would include the "little black dress" of silk, a black silk jersey hat and handbag of soft gathered black suede, cream doeskin gloves, and double strand of pearls. The ensemble might be finished with a cocktail handbag from France, made in softly draped black suede with black silky linings, and sold in Galeries Lafayette, which also had a branch in London. Black suede pouches gathered into an ivory frame with a suede handle, from Anglo-French bags, for example, were used on slightly more formal occasions.

But by 1953, cocktail bags were generally wafer thin, and many employed a new style of quilting. Tea dance and cocktail bags in handpainted satin were available from Wolfgang Brothers to accompany dresses of painted satin, while Italian-made cocktail bags in softest black gazelle added a feminine elegance, with their paste set mother-of-pearl and gilt frames.

By the end of the decade, the Sixties revolution was imminent. London designer Mary Quant had opened her first shop in 1955, and dresses began to get simpler and shorter. Box bags and pochettes had virtually disappeared, and as the formality of the 1950s began to fade, so straps on overarm bags began to lengthen.

This white box bag has a white plastic hinged lid and bottom, while the body is cardboard, covered with brocade and tiny silver beads. The handle is perspex.

Multi-colored 1960s clutch (*right*) with Chinese-style embroidery.

Clutching the Pochette

The strapless clutch bag was born out of the pochette of the 20s, which in turn evolved from the soft, fabric Dorothy bag of the century's first decade.

1950s silk bag (*above*), made in Japan. It is covered with tiny white and transparent beads in subtle, swirling patterns.

The pochette, later known as the clutch bag, had its heyday in the 1920s, 1930s, and again in the 1950s. It evolved around 1916-20 out of soft fabric bags, a popular shape at the time which was generally carried in the hand. This led to a style for large purses, rather like frame bags without the handle, and from these emerged the simple, rectangular pochettes, or "underarm" purses. Some designs incorporated a flat strap through which to slip the wrist or thumb for extra security.

By the 1920s, pochettes were slim and flat, some fastened with a simple twist-knob or streamlined slide catch, others with a zipper. Their elegant, uncluttered surfaces provided a smooth expanse for appliquéd or embroidered decoration, which often took the form of typical Art Deco geometric patterns and Egyptian-style motifs.

Specialist bag and accessory stores evolved in the U.S., such as Lilly Daché in New York, which sold custom-made or take-away accessories, including pocketbooks. Nat Lewis was the top New York store for bags at the time, while Koret, a specialized bagmaker, started up in the 1920s.

Before long, the pochette was the dominant handbag style for both day and evening wear, its smooth surfaces reflecting the dominant fashion trends of each decade. In the 1930s, the svelte, feminine look was emphasized, with pochettes made in a variety of expensive and exotic reptile skins, from dimpled ostrich leather to suede. Plain silk pochettes for night were enhanced with sparkling paste clips and clasps, or jeweled monograms. Others were made in gold and silver kid, or luxuriously beaded.

Fabric was often used—flowered crêpe summer dresses were often teamed with a matching pochette—especially during the austere war years, when many bags were homemade. Most of these were a

In the mid 1930s (right), the clutch bag was in its heyday; this one is in washable Pyralin.

simple envelope shape, crafted out of felt or satin for evenings, enhanced with a brooch or pin, or canvas and cotton for summer.

The pochette generally fell out of favor during the 1940s, however, as more practical shoulder bags took center stage. But it resurfaced in the 1950s as the clutch bag, held tightly in the hand or clutched closely to the body. It was particularly favored in Europe as it complemented both the narrow, tailored silhouette and the full skirted Dior look of the time. Elegant and simple, for both day and night, it was a neat, streamlined accessory for the feminine 1950s, and often worn with matching shoes.

Most clutches were variations on the rectangle, but there were some exceptions. One made by Bembaron, and sold at Harrods in 1954, was the shape of a doubled-up saucer. The American bag designer Ronay made large handbags with matching clutches in black, soft-ribbed faille, an idea that was followed in later

years by, among others, Lou Taylor and Donna Karan.

Exaggeratedly long clutch bags were first seen in Paris in the early 1960s, although small, simple envelope clutches remained popular for evening use. Rhinestone-studded versions could be bought from Jeanne Lanvin's boutique in Paris, while black ciré clutch bags patterned with roses were made by Enger Kress at Saks Fifth Avenue.

Although the clutch bag had little place among the radical fashions of the 1960s, it was reintroduced towards the end of the decade, thanks to a brief revival of 1930s style. Its form changed slightly for the early 1970s, turning into a soft, flat envelope bag produced in supple russet suede by Carrano or covered in golden scales, by Adrien Mann for evening wear. Distinguished designers, from St. Laurent to

Britain's Nigel Lofthouse for Jean Muir, designed appliqué leather clutches, while Clive Shilton's glazed, pastel kid, shell shapes were highly sought. But as clutches became larger and too big to be carried in the hand, they took on a sturdier aspect. Mulberry made them out of quilted tan and khaki leather in 1978.

In the early 1980s, it appeared in myriad forms, from the shocking pink-and-black-spotted, plastic envelopes by Jump Accessories, featured in the British teen magazine *Honey*, to Chanel's quilted clutches with rhinestones sparkling in each indentation, in 1984.

A proliferation of styles and shapes from chain stores and top designers included little beaded clutch bags worn both day and night in the late 1990s, and a range of subtle clutches in stone, taupe, and beige.

S. Launer & Company

The Queen of England, Elizabeth II, is rarely seen without a classic Launer bag over her arm. The company certainly does not consider itself to be part of high fashion. Its smart, clean elegant designs continually evolve, with the merest nod to the fashions of the day.

Sleek style (*above*), from the 1970 International Collection.

The concept of a small, multi-use, elegant bag like the 1970s example (*above*) was revolutionary.

Launer 's general philosophy focuses on form, function, and quality. It has been making bags for over 50 years, and was first established by a Czechoslovakian refugee, Sam Launer, who escaped to London from the Nazis during World War II. He set up the company in London's East End in 1941 and ran it until his death in the late 1960s, when his son took over. Although there are no Launers left now, the company continues to run, headed by Gerald Bodmer.

Today, Launer bags are made in one of their two factories, one in Hackney and one in the West Midlands, which employ around 38 people. Highly skilled craftsmen and women piece together the designs turned out by the company's in-house designers (there is currently a team of five, although the ultimate responsibility for the designs lies with the managing

director). In the past, some bags used over 100 pieces, although this number has been reduced over recent years, thanks to simpler designs, made mostly in smooth, gleaming calf, but also in reptile and ostrich skins. Great care is taken in selecting the materials.

Making each bag involves four main stages, and at least two people work on each one. The leather and lining suede are cut by hand from patterns, and then skived, or reduced in thickness around the edges, so that it can be turned and stitched. Once cut and prepared, the bag is stitched together, mainly by machine, and then polished to a high finish with oils. Finally, each bag is stamped in gold with the royal warrant "By Appointment to Her Majesty Queen Elizabeth II." Each bag is suede-lined and fitted with pockets and dividers, with as much attention being paid to

Shades of difference in shape and size (*left*), polished finish and the gold-plated brass, twisted rope fastening,

dresser visits Launer and chooses from their existing range, which also includes clutch and shoulder strap bags. Launer make alterations to her specifications, such as lengthening or shortening the handle. The Queen has also in the past bought bags for Princess Margaret, Princess Anne, and other members of the royal family. The Queen Mother is often seen carrying an old Launer bag which she has had for years. Launer handbags have a suitably royal, dignified, and understated appproach to fashion. For the Queen, accessories are chosen with public appearances in mind, and for their ability not to court controversy. For daily use, the Queen favors simple black or white, and occasionally taupe, although they are also available in navy, burgundy, brown, and beige. Their only embellishment is the trademark small gold-plated brass fastening, in a twisted rope design.

The Queen's fondness for Launer handbags goes beyond that of the public arena, to sheer practicability. Apparently, when asked by the wife of actor Roger Moore why she always carried a handbag in Buckingham Palace, she replied that it was because the palace was so large.

the bag's interior as its exterior, and can take anywhere from 2 1/2 to 5 hours to make. and a maker will probably work on 10-12 bags per week. Launer also make purses, wallets and belts and are about to launch a range of scarves. Since many of their exports are to places like Japan and the Paciific Rim, the handbags have to stand up to such climates. Many tests are carried out on new designs, for example how much weight the top handle bag will carry, how well it will survive in various climates and conditions, and how well it will perform over a long period of time.

Royal Service

The style favored by the Queen is square shaped, capacious and flap-fronted, with a top strap. The contents of the Queen's handbag are a closely guarded secret, although, famously, she never carries any money in it. S.

Launer & Co. were granted the Royal Warrant in the late 1960s, and they continue to supply the Palace today. The Queen possesses many Launer handbags, although they do not actually create bespoke bags exclusively for her. The Queen's

Handle-less clutch (*below*) from the 1970s collection made exclusively for the London department store, Harrods.

A pair of dainty clutch bags (*left*) from the 1996 collection.

1994 gift box bag (*above*) in black and white taffeta.

Lulu Guinness

Lulu Guinness is one of a small group of British handbag designers of the 90s, whose strengths lie in individuality of design and quality of craftsmanship. Their products fall, in style and affordability, somewhere between haute couture and the mass market.

Golden satin snap-shut bag (*above*), from Lulu Guinness's 1994 collection.

Following in the footsteps of earlier handbag designers such as the 1960s maker Sally Jess, who had worked as an actress, Lulu Guinness broke into the fashion world with no previous training. Her first design, in 1989, was for the "Lulu", a leather briefcase organizer with numerous pockets which she designed for herself, to help " compartmentalize her life" while she worked as a video production assistant in Paris.

The colorful suede, drawstring "dolly" bags which came next were soon being sold in great numbers in Liberty in London, and it was not long before Guinness found her true creative direction as "the Queen of evening bags". Her tiny bucket shapes in scarlet and pink silk grosgrain were an instant success, followed by leather pill box shapes which dangled from wrist-straps and circular, zipper topped bags in gleaming satin or suede. Her elegant and idiosyncratic creations fitted in with a new

femininity in fashion and were soon stocked by all the key high fashion London stores such as Harrods, Liberty, Joseph, and Browns.

Classic Status

Guinness's whimsical English look was also noticed by overseas buyers from Bergdorf Goodman, Nieman Marcus, and Saks Fifth Avenue in New York. Suzy Menkes, fashion editor for the *International Herald Tribune,* noted in 1995 the "dainty brocade purses, straw bucket bags, and madcap creations shaped like a pet pooch, so that you can look as though a shi-tzu (it unzips at the top) is tucked under your arm." Guinness agreed that the "Lap Dog", a chenille trimmed clutch dog bag with tartan bow, would suit only a "very particular person," but commented that her "Florist's Basket" had a wider appeal.

An exquisite, bucket-shaped satin bag, barely 4 inches (10 cm) square, the loop handled lid of the Florist's Basket was covered with velvet roses.

The Florist's Basket, in black satin with velvet roses, is on permanent display at London's Victoria & Albert Museum.

striped grosgrain bags to ruched ribbon sacks and buckets, and has helped to reintroduce a feeling of glamor into the world of bags. "A few months ago, people used their jeans pockets to carry taxi fares and cigarettes. Now they come to me with their Manolo Blahnik slippers and ask me for a satin bucket to match," she is quoted as saying.

Not content with appealing to celebrities and collectors, Guinness recently joined a group of bright young British accessory designers who include the bagmaker Bill Amberg and milliner Phillip Treacy. Together, they produce an exclusive range of accessories for Debenhams, a middle-of-the-range, British department store, which included beaded and fringed velvet bags.

Lulu Guinness may not have had formal training, but her bags have brought a new freshness and vivacity to the world of accessories.

This bag has attained the status of a design classic and is in the permanent collection of bags in London's Victoria & Albert Museum. Other versions included baskets in purple, black, or chocolate velvet with purple or ivory violets. Guinness stated that, "I tend to design a flower bag each season and this one was created to go with the Jane Austen look of Empire-line dresses and country-cottage flowers. Violets are an old-fashioned flower and velvety in appearance and feel."

More recent designs include suede shoppers or totes and the "baby bag" for style-conscious mothers, in a black and gold Celia Birtwell print, which was sold by mail order. Guinness's designs pay tribute to the formality of 1950s styling, from her early, boxy,

An evening clutch bag (below) inspired by the pochettes of the 1920s.

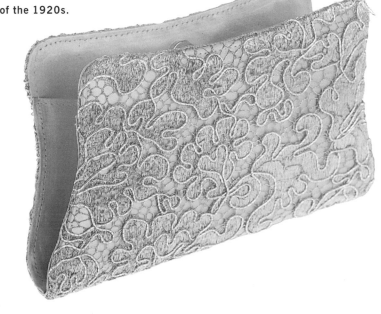

The Swinging Sixties

The 1960s, a decade of extremes, was summed up by two films released at the beginning of the decade. Fellini's *La Dolce Vita* gloried in the good times that had arrived with the European recovery from war, while Hitchcock's tense thriller, *Psycho*, hinted at a darker, more violent undercurrent. The fashion world mirrored this split personality. Clothes and accessories early in the decade reflected a lingering formality from the 1950s — large overarm bags were still all the rage — but became bold and experimental in the mid 1960s, accompanied by outrageous face and body make-up. Evening dress effusively decorated with beads, glitter, and plastics were echoed by evening bags in the same vein. Twiggy (*left*) shot to fame as the blue-eyed British beauty whose blank look skyrocketed her to becoming one of the richest models in the world.

Seventeen-year-old Leslie "Twiggy" (*above*) Hornby strikes a "leggy" pose wearing a mini skirt in 1966, London. A typical 1960s day bag (*right*) - possibly inspired by the Kelly bag - made of snakeskin with a black patent flap.

Jane Fonda, another icon of the period, attends the 1967 Venice Film Festival with her then-husband Roger Vadim. She is carrying a small evening clutch bag embroidered with flowers.

TEENAGE REBELS

The 1960s were a time of exploration — Yuri Gagarin became the first man in space in 1961 — and also a time of social turmoil. The Berlin Wall went up in 1961, and the world was stunned by the assassinations of President Kennedy in 1963 and Martin Luther King Jr. and Robert Kennedy in 1968. America in particular was struck by race riots and dissent over its involvement in the Vietnam War, which reached its peak in 1968. But above all, the 1960s were notable for the development of a youth culture. The voice of the teenager made itself heard in social and fashion issues, epitomized by the wild success of the British pop group, the Beatles, who inspired mass hysteria in the early 1960s. Their trouser suits of 1963, designed by French designer Pierre Cardin and still remarkably conventional, were widely influential on street fashions of the time.

In 1966, a growing peace movement developed against all the violence of the age, led by the young. The drug-influenced popular art of the movement — which showed in its music and clothes — soon became known as psychedelic. Psychedelic art was easily recognized by its distinctive, colorful swirled patterns, which covered everything, from wallpaper to album covers, and carrier bags. The peace movement culminated in the Woodstock festival of peace and love in 1969 held in America, but in Britain too, music had became the domain of youth, and a powerful influence on fashion.

Street Style Rules

No longer was fashion exclusively determined by the couture houses. Instead, and for the first time, small boutiques and street styles run by non-couture designers such as London's Mary Quant influenced the fashion houses. Mary Quant opened her first shop in 1955, and started her influential Ginger Group label in 1963. All her clothes were accompanied by a range of accessories, which were an inexpensive way to instantly update one's look, and break the established rules of fashion.

Quant's first bags were made in black and white PVC, decorated either with big dots or with her famous daisy motif. They had long thin shoulder straps or chains, and were fastened with zippers. As she wrote in her autobiography *Quant on Quant*, published in 1966, "It is said that I was first with knickerbockers, gilt chains, shoulderstrap bags and high boots...I want to invent new ways of making clothes in new

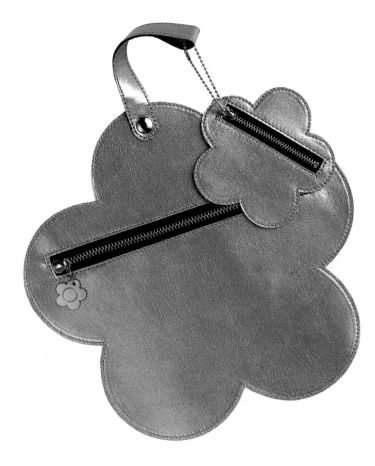

Silver leather wrist bag (*left*) by Mary Quant is in her characteristic daisy motif which featured extensively on her clothes, accessories, and make-up.

A chic black patent leather bag with a stylish chrome twist clasp, set in a diamond-shape motif, was made in France during the early 1960s. The single handle can be held or worn over the arm.

materials, with new shapes and new fashion accessories that are up to date with the changing ways of life."

New York was full of similar boutiques, most in the Greenwich Village area of the city, while department stores such as Bergdorf Goodman installed a boutique of their own inside the larger store to cater for a younger clientele. One chain of department store boutiques was 'Anne Klein Corners,' found in major department stores across the country; they sold Anne Klein designs and accessories, which became increasingly important to Klein's overall look.

The fashionable ideal for women became younger and younger as the decade continued, exemplified by the childlike British model Twiggy, with her doe-eyed make-up and knock-kneed stance. The dress silhouette became shorter, cut far above the knee by 1965, and ever more minimal, taking the form of sleeveless, straight dresses without a waistline. Many clothes fashions fell into one of two categories of design. On the one hand, futuristic and graphic textile designs influenced by Op-Art (the term comes from a shortening for 'optical') were seen in the outfits of Pierre Cardin, Ungaro, and Yves St Laurent, while a combination of psychedelic, ethnic, and antique influences also eventually filtered into designer collections. This heralded the approach of a new romanticism in fashion, and by the late 1960s, the mini skirt was in decline; the longer maxi and midis finally began to win over.

In the first few years of the 1960s, handbags were still enormous and mainly overarm, with short, firm, single or double handles. Bamboo was still much used for handles in the early 1960s, seen in full circles in a black crocodile carryall from Cartier, while Claude Javelet in Paris employed brass to make his bracelet handles.

On the whole, handbags were triangular at the base, narrow in width, and longer than they were wide. One example, from Susan of Knightsbridge, London, came in glossy brown calf, edged with black stitching, with a flapped pocket on the outside of the bag to provide easy access to train tickets or make-up.

The simple all-in-one bag with a cutout handle that was so typical of the 1960s began to appear as early as 1961. By 1964, relaxed suede bags by the Italian firm of Gucci had an integral

The minimal chic of Oleg Cassini

In the early 1960s, icon of femininity for American women, First Lady Jaqueline Kennedy, was dressed primarily by Oleg Cassini. He was appointed official designer to the First Lady and was responsible for her expensive but simple look which became an instant classic, copied by many women. The accessories — pill box hat, plain shoes, white gloves, small amounts of jewelry, and a small, matching envelope bag — were as significant as the clothes themselves. Oleg Cassini became so successful that he branched out into many other areas of fashion by 1963, and today his company still produces accessories of many kinds, including handbags.

A Japanese 1960s wooden bead bag has a strap made of beads and a cheap metal chain. The strap is attached to the bag with large metal rings, and an elasticated bead loop fastens the bag.

shoulder strap, while a year later the former British actress-turned-handbag designer Sally Jess was designing bags of white leather, the top simply tapering to a handle.

The Return of the Shoulder bag

With some exceptions, handbag designers lagged behind their peers in the fashion world, and many of the classic overarm bags looked wrong with the new zappy 1960s fashions. This was suddenly resolved in 1964 with the arrival of the shoulder bag.

The sling-strap bag, "bag of the year," as American *Vogue* called it, was exceedingly versatile. There were long chain straps, mid-length straps, double straps which could be used to carry the bag on the shoulder or in the hand, and even overarm bags that were meant to be worn on the shoulder. "Over the shoulder bags in white textured leather with swagger pockets look marvellous with black and white tweeds, the ringed strap adjusts to any length," enthused one journalist about a range of MM's bags on sale at Saks Fifth Avenue.

But bags soon had to become smaller, as oversized models were impractical. Before long, chain link strap bags were being made by Greta at Bonwit Teller, and Fassbender & Evens' produced a lizard patterned calf or silk envelope slung on a gilt chain. It was designed to hang from the shoulder, although the chain also doubled up as handles. This shrinking in size was also taken to extremes, and the no-bag handbag developed, to sling over the shoulder and forget about. Wallet-sized bags of corduroy and leather with gilt studs and black snaps were made by the British manufacturer Russell & Bromley, among others, in 1964, designed to be worn with trousers, skirts, or coats. By 1965, all bags were smaller, and the gilt handled "little black bag" became popular in Paris. As handbags got smaller they held less and less, and in the end, not enough. One solution was to put two compartments back to back, to make one bag.

A very elegant day or evening bag made from chain mail of tiny white enameled squares lined in purple silk taffeta. The handle is a flexible chain-link cord, also in white enamel.

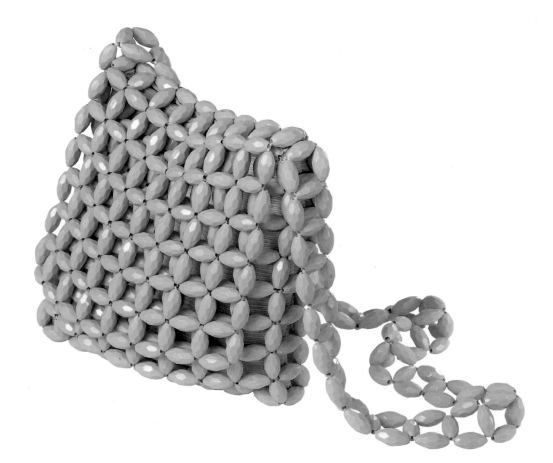

A small unstructured shoulder bag made of large, brightly colored turquoise glass beads. Italian made, it represents the confidence of 1960s youth culture, which was absorbed by mainstream manufacturers.

Examples from Bagatelle Bags were made in white leather, with long chain linked shoulder straps, and went on sale in Bloomingdales. Their success encouraged other similar models, and such bags soon began to be almost as wide as they were tall, featured in fashion magazines with both trouser suits and sleeveless summer dresses.

MATERIAL CHANGES

The typical, large overarm bag with flap front and gilt fastening received much of its decorative interest from the patterning of exotic skins, real or fake. Charles Jourdan's large, deep honey-blond crocodile bag of 1961, with its single handle and gilt finished strap fastening, was typical of formal daywear, while his smart and capacious black suede and patent shoppers brought style to casual wear.

Pigskin, used repeatedly in the 1940s and 1950s to make typically sturdy country shoulder bags with brass detail, was now widely employed to make town bags. It was suitable for the large and substantial styles of the early 1960s, for which softer, more pliable leathers would have been impractical. Such bags were finished with gleaming, simple fittings, with business-like briefcase fastenings enhanced with the odd decorative buckle or two.

Fashionable overarm bags were also made in solid fabrics such as tweed and tartan. Many had leather trimmings, such as those by Francis Winter for Cosserat in Paris, which also had gleaming button and press stud fastenings, and double flaps. In America, the tradition of saddlestitching continued on bags made by St. Thomas of New York in their Mellotouch Cowhide, which

An archetypal 1960s bag for day or evening from Italy. Large chrome discs mounted on woven silver sacking form the body and the large chrome ring handles are attached by silver leather. Paco Rabanne-inspired, this bag celebrates the use of space age materials.

Capacious cream patent leather bag (*far right*) features a large front flap, short single handle and brass fittings. The bag was made in France for Fior in 1967. A white leather day bag from the early 1960s (*right*), unusually, features a watch on a buckled strap inset into the center of the front panel.

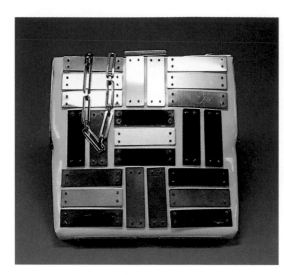

Pierre Cardin bag (*above*)
from the 1960s is a
patchwork of metallic strips
and chain link strap.
A Paco Rabanne bag made of
linked silver-colored metal
and white plastic discs
(*below left*) fastens with a
hinged metal clasp. Another
unusual use of material is
evident in the silver-colored
plastic bag (*below right*)
made in the U.S. during the
late 1960s.

came with a range of matching leather accessories from purses and cigarette cases to billfolds and more.

By 1964, the blurring of social conventions was represented by dark green suede, town and country bags from Gucci. These had rounded flaps and topstitching, and combined flexibility with the substantial look of the handbags of the day. There was an increasing need for a bag that allowed the wearer to take advantage of the social freedoms of the 1960s, and women were experimenting with the bags at their disposal. Spectator sports bags from Russell & Bromley in ribbed corduroy, like buckled satchels, were worn by girls-about-town, for example.

Fabric bags were seen in any number of guises, from Etienne Aigner's rather formal matching shoes and handbags in continental linen and leather available in 1961 to their 1967 fishnet patterned bags — fishnet was experiencing another vogue as a material for pantihose. Synthetic fabrics were used in ranges such as a "Glove Mates" spectacular by Hansen, a cable stitch set of gloves, hat and bag in 100% Orlon acrylic, while in London in 1960, swinging young fashions were beginning to transform the late 1950s duffel coat into huge shoulder bags big enough to hold records or books.

As the "flower power" movement gathered momentum, flowers began to be sprinkled across accessories and furnishings. By 1965, they were seen everywhere, adorning buttons, tights, and even flowered Dick Whittington bags which could be bought from Galeries Lafayette. It was even possible to order envelope bags in flowery patterns on thin gilt chains from Susan Handbags in London, to match summer dresses.

The Classic Evening Bag

The early years of the decade saw conventional shapes and decoration on evening bags; purses in glossy patent were thought smart for the young. In America, cocktail handbags of "inspired design", Tesoros by Tano of Madrid, were imported from Spain. They were decorated with true color reproductions of Old Master paintings.

Mesh bags from Whiting & Davis were still highly sought, the fake mother of pearl frames of their Oromesh bags of 1961 studded with rhinestones, and the body made

of silver or gold colored mesh. Good quality main street evening bags in gold mesh bags were also provided by Adrien Mann. Slim envelopes covered in gold and silver beading were available from Asprey of London's Bond Street store, while in 1963, the very wealthy could buy black satin evening bags with 18 carat gold frames set with diamonds.

As evening wear became bold and experimental in the mid 1960s, so too did evening bags become more adventurous in design. Such inspiration was perhaps clearest in imitation of Paco Rabanne's mini dresses of 1965, many of which utilized man-made materials in a decorative, three-dimensional way. Among the most distinctive was his mini dress made of giant plastic discs.

A cheerful plastic summer bag or vanity case (*left*) made by Lily Pulitzer Inc. in the 1960s. The plastic is covered with cotton and ribbon and patchworked together.

A white summer basket, profusely decorated with plastic flowers, and ribbon threaded through the weave. The lid lifts up and fastens with a metal catch.

Casual Day Bags

Solid large bags in sensible shades of brown, black, and taupe were seen everywhere early in the decade, featured by stores and manufacturers such as Eugenie Buchner, Lederer, and the British shoe and bag chain store Russell and Bromley, which had provided affordable bags of quality and good design for decades. In 1962, they launched a range of huge pigskin bags, while Woollands, also of London, made huge, flat, satchel bags of soft goat leather copied from Paris. They had a short flap with a special make-up pouch inside.

In 1962 capacious Gladstone bags were popular, while American *Vogue* of 1964 featured "stand-up and be counted accessories" that included distinctive handbags of tawny tiger, lizard, and saffian leather, such as a shiny black saffian envelope with gilt and bamboo handle by Koret. A tawny, stripy tiger handbag from Nettie Rosenstein in New York was "almost large enough to stash a telescopic sight," and

The extended clutch bag

In 1960, the French edition of *Vogue* featured a plain, narrow clutch bag, or pochette, on its cover which was twice the length of most such bags. A series of equally extreme designs followed, made in dark flannel and smooth calf, some flap fronted and others closed with zippers. This Parisian fashion for exceptionally long clutches found its way to Britain and then America, where such "handbags of lengthy dachshund proportions," as American *Vogue* referred to them in 1961, provided an equally large alternative to the fashionably outsized overarm bag of the day.

The success of the design proved that clutch bags were still attractive to women with an eye for fashion, and wide, top fastening bags with short handles soon followed, such as one in grey flannel by Florsheim. The British firm Susan of Knightsbridge made a range of smart, framed pochettes in tortoiseshell and black patent, while the young British designer Jane Shilton made many smooth, long calf pochettes that picked up on the Parisian dachshund idea in the early 1960s. For the younger set, purse-shaped clutches in glossy patent or pastels, or trimmed with flower shaped clasps, reflected the youthful fashions of the day.

Actress Audrey Hepburn walks hand-in-hand with her husband, Andrea Dotti along Rome's fashionable Via Condotti. She carries a Kelly bag, the bag of the moment.

was gusseted and handled in black calfskin, while in 1964 French designer, Lucille, made huge, sleek envelopes of beige French lizard, with snaky latches.

In 1961, as the accessory market expanded, Nettie Rosenstein had moved from dressmaking to creating accessories and handbags. She was not alone, as many dress designers turned to accessories as the 1960s progressed. One was the American designer Bonnie Cashin, who eventually won the Leather Industries American Handbag Designer Award in 1968. As the return of the shoulder bag gathered momentum, ostrich skin was often used. In America in 1967, Neiman-Marcus created little ostrich bags to "swing through Spring" in the latest fashion colors, including shocking pink. A brief fashion for fur in 1967 saw giraffe, pony, and leopard skin inset shoulder strap bags.

In 1964, futuristic shapes and materials were all the rage, and PVC, metallic surfaces, geometric designs and cut outs were employed by designers old and new. The Paris design house of André Courrèges highlighted silver and white in his clothes and used unconventional materials, seen in his short vinyl dresses and kneelength boots.

Bag designers took up the call, and in 1966, Sally Jess's simple flat silver kid bag with clearcast perspex handles and zipper closing became one of the first to fit in with

Up to date with color

Early in the 1960s, bags and shoes were still commonly teamed up to provide an organized, rather formal look. Magazines gave advice on matching accessories, as they had done in the 1950s, emphasizing the importance of keeping up with the many new colors that were introduced. "Catch on to the new color wavelengths with the right balance of toning . . . everything from top to toe must shine as good as new, be up to date, in fact, with it, all the way," wrote *Vogue* in 1961 - a year in which Clove Carnation, Peat Brown and French Mustard were the colors to be seen in.

A slim, elegant dress bag of antelope skin and faux pearl and gold metal clasp (above *left*), was made in the very early 1980s by Fior in Italy, and reflects the quality and elegance of that country's leather goods. The bright red travel bag (above *right*) of calf leather, accompanied by a change purse, is also made by Fior, this time in England. A late 1960s Fior bag (*bottom*) displays a wide opening, substantial handles, and a weighty buckle.

A bag for vacation

Back in the 1950s, the vacation bag market had been cornered by Italian straw bags, which had become synonymous with the vacation spirit. This trend continued into the following decade, seen in 1960 in Simonetta of Rome's huge flat woven straw bag with fringes and bamboo top and handles, which was worn with a large straw hat.

By 1964, the best dressed women carried beach bags shaped like an Ali Baba jar from Liberty. These were made of strong green straw, and were tall and capacious. Liberty imported many interesting artefacts but their own designs were also distinctive, with bags made from their own Liberty lawns and printed silks. One 1964 bag in shades of turquoise was gathered onto a bamboo handle and sold with a matching scarf.

Baku straw handbags made in the shape of a Panama hat, on chain handles, were sold from Henri Bétrix on Madison Avenue in 1967, while jute bags with teak handles were imported from the Far East by "Exotic Imports Inc." of California. For those who wanted more locally made products, hand crocheted raffia totes "in 11 swingy colors" were available from Takahashi in San Francisco.

A floral printed satin bag, shaped rather like a make-up bag, lined with pink plastic. The floral print reflects the popularity of 1960s "flower power" styling.

the Space Age look. Worn with fishnet patterned silver stockings and cut out silver shoes, they were available from Countdown, a boutique on London's King's Road. Designer bags included a starkly simple, neon orange shoulder bag from Pierre Cardin, the latest in handbags in Paris in 1966, and Paco Rabanne's chainmail bags, made from overlapping plastic discs. Huge white bags with a circular cutout for the handle, in shiny patent or PVC, reflected the styling on shoes in 1966. Gleaming white vinyl bags, long and narrow on a lean, white plastic linked shoulder chain, were a 1967 creation from the startling shoe designer Roger Vivier.

By the late 1960s, the exploration of space and the rapid development of plastics and manmade materials inspired a plethora of neon-lit, futuristic fashion shots, such as those by the American designer Giorgio di Sant' Angelo for Diana Vreeland, editor of *Vogue* from 1963–71. The look was not for everyone, however. Established handbag manufacturers continued to make classic bags for older women, and couture designers such as Mainbocher accessorized their wealthy clients in pearls, white gloves, plain pumps, and matching handbags. But the fashions of youth were dominant, reflecting in turn the romantic concerns of the realms of inner space, the psychedelia of free expression, and a nostalgia for the past.

A well-designed American evening bag (*above*) made by Whiting and Davis, of large, silver-colored metal mesh, with a stylish, molded Perspex handle. .

A very elegant two tone classic envelope bag by Kurt Geiger (*left*), features a simple handle and twist clasp.

How to jazz up a simple Kelly bag (*below*); this two-tone geometric design is by Goldpfeil.

The Kelly Bag

Square, conservative, and functional, the "Kelly" bag acquired its name and movie star status when it was carried by the actress Grace Kelly the day she married Prince Rainier of Monaco.

A variation of the Kelly bag, not from the original Hermès stable, but by British designer Patrick Cox

The wedge-shaped Kelly bag, called the "small tall bag with straps" by its creator Hermès, first appeared in 1935. It was a refinement of an earlier, larger "tall bag with straps" which Hermès launched in 1932 as a saddlebag. The distinctive Kelly bag of today is still, in effect, a saddlebag reduced in scale.

Until 1955, the "small tall bag with straps" was known as the Hermès, but it was rechristened the Kelly bag by Hermès on the occasion of Grace Kelly's marriage to Prince Rainier of Monaco. The bag received a further boost to its image when it was featured on the front cover of *Life* magazine in 1956, carried up front by the Princess, to, it was rumored, hide her pregnancy.

The Kelly has a number of distinguishing features, including its saddlestitching, a front fastening, and a padlock and rotating clasp with "Hermès-Paris" stamped on the lock. The bag's short double straps are placed in the centre of its sides, towards the top, and there is a removable shoulder strap which was first added in 1970.

Each Kelly bag is saddlestitched by hand at the Hermès premises at 24 Faubourg Saint Honoré, Paris, and to make a whole bag from start to finish can take their skilled employees anywhere between 15-20 hours.

Original Craftmanship
The process starts with selecting the skin—Kelly bags are made in box calf in all colors, canvas and leather, ostrich, horsehair, lizard, and crocodile. The material is cut into the necessary pieces. These are then glued together before the linings for the bag are prepared. All the different components are then assembled and saddlestitched before being polished and buffed to a fine finish. Finally, the clasp and gold Hermès symbol are attached to the bag's flap.

Within a few years of its arrival on the fashion scene, the Kelly went from

The traditional Kelly bag is now available in a wide spectrum of colors from both the original makers, Hermès, and other companies such as those below by Goldpfeil.

being a bag that Hermès could hardly sell, to an international fashion icon. Hermès have produced a number of variations on the original, the basic model of which stands 14 ins (35 cm) tall; the next size up is 16 ins (40 cm) tall. Kellys have appeared in a vivid array of colors, including lime green and sapphire blue (1994), the "Kellgo" of the same year, and the red "Kelly mou" of 1995.

Imitations

Unsurprisingly, the bag's huge success has led to endless imitations and tributes. There are mass-produced versions made and sold by chain stores, competitive models by major designers, such as Patrick Cox with his bright green, patent leather Kelly bag of 1995, plastic Kellys, and even grunge versions. Helen Taylor's Kelly bags made from recycled candlewick bedspreads and chenille curtains of 1994, from London's Portobello Road, fall into this last category.

Despite the hundreds of copies available at a fraction of the price, Hermès's order books are always full. There is a long waiting list for each bag, but its durability more than makes up for the wait—in fact, the bags are thought to improve with age. Many Hermès clients are remarkably faithful to the company, returning their bags to the Fauborg St Honoré for the complimentary repolish that Hermès offers, or for a rehaul or reconditioning. Imitators may refer to their copies as look-alikes, but the Kelly is a protected style, and legal action is taken against imitators to ensure its continuing exclusivity. For a design whose origins lie in a humble saddlebag, the Kelly has inspired devotion and imitation in equal measure.

The House of Hermès

Classic Hermès style (*above*).

Hermès successfully adapted and refined the saddlemaker's skills to create a range of sturdy, voluminous bags that marry classic style and function.

"Kelly à dos" (backpack) (*above*) **by Frederic Dumas for Hermès.**

The great house of Hermès was founded in 1837 by a leather worker, Emile-Charles Hermès. He worked as a harness- and saddlemaker, supplying the carriagemakers of the Champs-Elysées and the great stables of France with such success that in the 1880s he transferred his business to 24 rue Faubourg St Honoré, in the heart of Paris.

The family business was by now extremely successful, and concentrated on selling equestrian equipment to private customers. With the advent of the motor car, and the consequent demise of the horsedrawn carriage, Hermès applied the exceptiona leatherworking skills that the company had developed over the years to new areas. The company began to make wallets, traveling cases, and handbags, using the same saddlestitching techniques that had been so crucial in making top quality saddles and harnesses.

In 1917, there was another radical change to the company's product line. On a trip to Canada, Emile Hermès saw the relatively new zip fastener used to seal the roof of a motor car. On his return to France, he secured an exclusive patent and launched the Bugatti bag, fastened with a zipper which came to be known as the "Hermès closure".

Bags of Distinction

Since the 1930s, Hermès have produced a series of classic bag designs, each in keeping with its time. The 1942, functional, capacious Market bag for shopping reflected wartime preoccupations but was far more elegant than the average clumsy wartime bag.

The launch, in the 1950s, of the large Kelly bag—which was to become one of the most successful bags of the 20th century—was a coup for the company. Stars such as Marlene Dietrich, Grace Kelly and Ingrid Bergman flocked to Hermès in search of stylish luxury through the 1950s and 1960s. A typical Hermès handbag "to outdistance all others in pure luxury" was made in pigskin with a deep front flap, and fastened with a square lock clasp. Two inner compartments were each lined in soft suede, and the matching diary case, refillable each year, had its own silver pencil.

More recent notable designs have included the "Birkin" and the "Bolide," a calfskin duffel bag in 1988, the small, "H" leather shoulder bag of 1990, and the 1994 Macpherson bag, named after supermodel Elle Macpherson. This large, Bugatti style bag has a clip-on base section for carrying make-up.

No matter what the design, from enormous tote bags, rigid leather bucket bags, shoulder bags in green felt and leather, to the 1997 asymmetrical shoulder bag, all Hermès products share a functional root, a boxy shape and an unfussy style. The result is a name associated with quality and collectibility, although many of the designs have been widely copied.

Even the distinctive wrapping, the zipper remembered in the "broken teeth" design along the edges of the brown ribbon which bind the famous orange Hermès box, inspire fetishistic delight. In an article in British *Vogue* in July 1995, Susan Irvine, an obsessive collector of empty Hermès boxes, writes: "My Hermès boxes are symbols. They stand for the peak of luxury, for a certain lifestyle. They are my dream boxes."

Hermès have always retained their philosophy of craftsmanship—there is no licensing and their products are closely controled—and the Hermès flagship remains in Paris, along with the Hermès Museum in the Faubourg Saint Honoré, where the collection of equestrian arts and paintings put together by the founder Emile-Charles is housed. Hermès are, of course, not only famous for their leather goods. Their richly designed silk twill squares, typically patterned with subjects such as carriages and horses, are also dear to the heart of the company. Production began in 1937 with the creation of *Les Jeux des Omnibus et des Dames Blanches*, and many of the original designs which followed have never gone out of production. Today, there are two collections a year, with roughly six designs per season. In the late 1950s, Hermès opened its perfume division under Jean Guerrand, launching Calèche in 1961, and the company has also branched out into other luxury items, such as porcelain, crystal, clocks, watches, jewelry, silverware, gloves, and diaries.

Black leather 1950s traveling bag (*below*) with burgundy interior and a hinged jewelry box at the base.

Capacious red leather handbag "Fedou" by Frédéric Dumas with punched leather logo.

Following the Sixties Radicals

The 1970s followed one of the most dynamic and directed decades in fashion, and as a result, the 70s are often viewed as less radical and interesting in terms of style and fashion. During the 1970s, those who had participated in the activism of the 1960s were now moving into positions of influence. There was a disaffection with couture, which seemed out of touch with what women really wanted, and many design cottage industries emerged during this time, encouraged by the alternative lifestyles begun in the 1960s. Feminism had become a serious issue, and fashion reflected this change in attitude. Bags for working women were seen everywhere as clothes styles moved away from the little girl look of the previous decade. Unisex, ethnic, new romantic, and casual looks all appeared during this decade, while the music world played an increasingly influential role in the fashions of the young.

American icon, Jackie Onassis (*above*), carries a casual straw basket while shopping on Capri. 1980s, bright, jazzy handbag (*right*) made of plastic discs and interwoven with metal—this bag is very reminiscent of Sixties psychedelia.

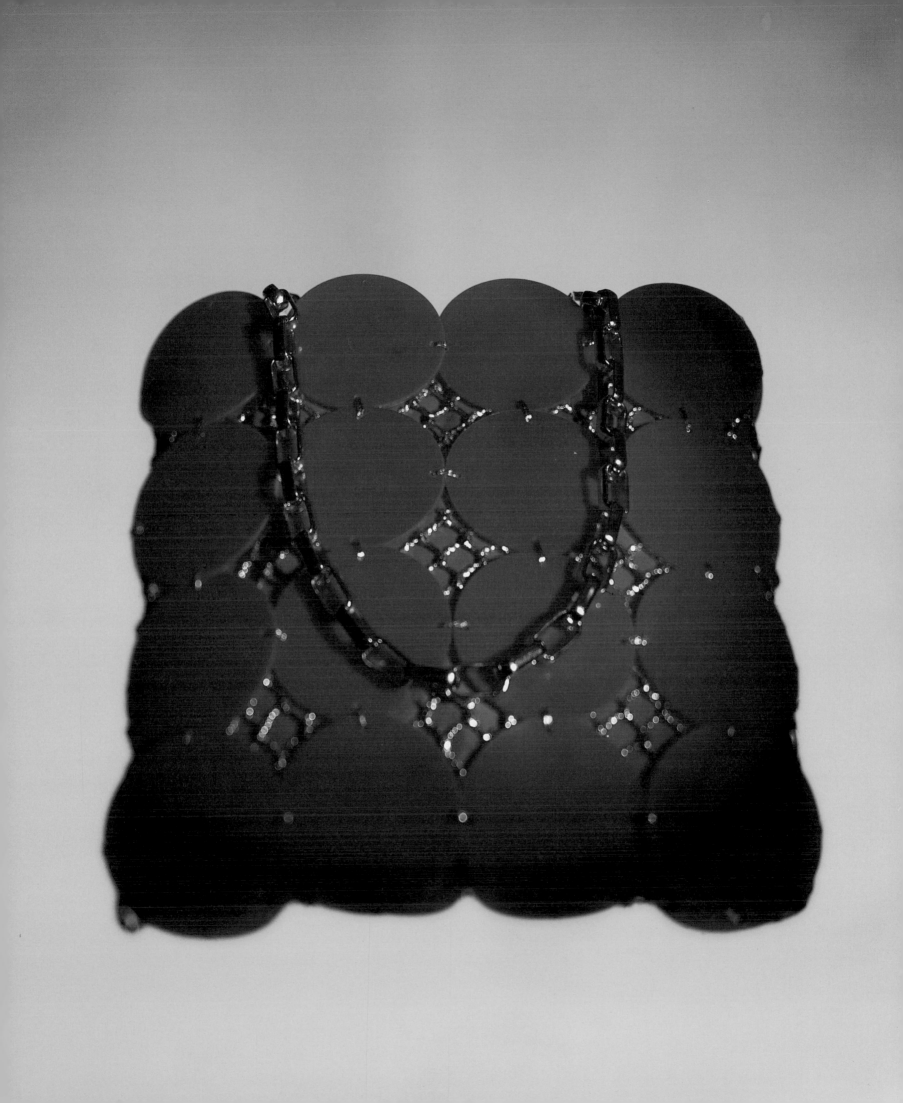

Jacobson's Michigan

Creamy-soft leather shirtcoat, a natural traveler by LEDASPAIN, Alabaster, gold or brown. 8 to 16 sizes. $210.

Working women demanded practical handbags that were functional as well as attractive during the 70s. Shoulderbags, like the one shown in this Jacobson's ad, proved to be very popular.

FASHION NOSTALGIA

Although the 1970s started out with a huge collection of available bag styles, by the end of the decade it was clear that a few dominant styles had ruled the decade. One of these, Yves St Laurent's tribute to the fashions of the 1940s, first appeared in 1971, with such accessories as platform soled shoes and boots worn alongside the shoulder bag. Not long afterwards, fashion nostalgia for the 1930s became apparent in the designs from the London store, Biba, with its bias cut dresses and clutch bags. This reflected a current delight in dressing up, as those interested in street fashions scoured markets and jumble sales for granny dresses and secondhand clothes. Battered, fabric shoulder bags and antique purses were avidly sought.

By 1975, the large, soft leather shoulder bag had joined the fashion parade, and went on to become the most significant handbag style of the decade, taking over from the fur bags, tiny shoulder purses, satchels, and army bags which had all had their moment.

Music had an enormous influence on the clothes and accessories worn by the young, especially following the legendary Woodstock Festival in 1969, where Jimi Hendrix and a host of others played and made music history. Shiny suits and make-up for men first made their appearance with the rise of glam rock, influenced by pop stars such as David Bowie, Queen, Elton John, and Abba, while Bruce Springsteen, Bob Marley, the Sex Pistols, and punk rock all spawned their own clothing styles.

Music and fashion became inextricably linked, and the divergence of older and youth styles became more marked. Few young women in the 1970s would be seen carrying a rigid overarm bag, for example, although such bags were being made.

Despite, or perhaps because of, the anti-war feeling of the time, military looking clothes and other accessories were snapped up from army surplus stores. By subverting army wear in this way, its aggressive associations were somehow weakened, and the young proudly wore their khaki shoulder bags with rivets and brass buckles, secondhand ammunition cases, and rucksacks, all of which could be bought at very low prices.

Clothes with Flare

As dress codes became less restrictive, and unisex fashions and jeans became adopted by nearly everybody, trouser suits with long, flared trousers were widely worn by women. Those with money invested in a trouser suit of wool or silk which could be worn both during the day and at night, accompanied by a leather

Patchwork patterns were very popular and this Fior turtleskin, patchwork bag, with substantial brass closings, trimmings, and clasps, made in 1974, would have been highly fashionable.

A black and white, fur shoulder bag with leather strap and zip closing, provides an example of the rather outlandish materials that were employed during the 1970s.

A jumble of styles

As the 1970s dawned, bags were available in an extraordinary range of styles and shapes. There were handbags in combinations of fur and reversed calf, leather, and webbing, and colorful patchworks of lizard-skin-dyed scarlet, orange, and green. Camera cases, cartridge cases, mail pouches, feed bags, bags strapped right under the arm, and bags hung on long straps were decorated with Moroccan studding and embroidery.

Fake python skin was trimmed with harness brass, while strips of suede were woven into chained leather bags. Perhaps most strangely of all, plaid sporran bags meant to be hung from the waist were designed by Thought Waves for Lewis Purses, at Bonwit Teller.

shoulder or clutch bag. Those with less to spend bought cheerfully colored 'loon' pants or invested in a pair of jeans. Denim accessories, sometimes embroidered with flowers, or decorated with brass studs, were made both at home and commercially, many making the most of the vogue for patchwork. Some shoulder bags were made out of pieces of patchwork denim, and others from patchwork leather.

Hemlines Migrate

Lengths of skirts varied enormously in the early 1970s, from the mini to the maxi, with the midi in between. Combinations of more than one length were often worn together, as in a brief 1971 fashion for hot pants in velvet and satin worn with maxi coats. Such outfits were sometimes accompanied by chunky overarm bags, but on the whole, the easy shoulder bag proved the most flexible solution to the lack of style consistency. In an era when tie-dyed T-shirts nestled up to cotton suede dresses, big, brimmed hats, and velvet cloches, only more pattern and softness looked right. Suede shoulder bags made by Lesley Slight for Peter Jones were typical, a 1971 example in grey and beige shades finished with a scalloped flap and topstitching, and a matching belt in appliqué. Very bright colors and clown make-up were fashionable in 1972, along with big watches, big sailor collars, tank tops, platform soles, and clogs. After dark, Pucci prints and fake fur topped off by appliqué and handpainted bags by Nigel Lofthouse and Biba were *de rigeur*.

The ethnic look was still going strong, with quilted Mao jackets and clothes made in Peru, North America, India, and the Middle East combined with home-made tie-dye fabrics, blue jeans, rainbow-hued shoes with chunky soles, leather midi skirts, caftans, and checked bandana scarfs. Embroidered and woven shoulder bags were seen everywhere, as were capacious carpet bags slung on leather straps from 1976 on.

A peacock motif, embroidered in gold thread on a black velvet background, decorates a 1970s evening bag.

Very much an ethnic-hippy style bag, it is made of brown, wooden beads, constructed in a diagonal pattern. It closes with a large bead and loop.

The huge success of the boutiques of the 1960s had depended on their providing the accessories to accompany the latest street fashions. In so doing, they provided a selling point for the many small home industries that made such items. A kind of fashion self-sufficiency took root, as people assembled outfits that were unique to them, making the most of homely skills such as knitting, patchwork, and appliqué. Working with leather and suede was popular, sometimes with brass studs, and dresses, skirts, jackets, and accessories, including unstructured handbags, could be made by anyone with a sewing machine.

In Britain and America, markets crammed with stalls selling such goods sprung up, especially in London and on the West Coast of America. Many small businesses later expanded into importing Indian and other ethnic goods. In America, embroidered shoulder bags were made by Gail van der Hoofe for Allen Cole Boutique, beaded bags and belts made to order by "Vicki and Jo," and Maxine Clement's appliqué bags in New York came from Henri Bendel.

Keeping Up with the Clutch

In 1972, in keeping with the 1930s revival, British *Vogue* declared the soft, flat envelope "bag of the year." Nigel Lofthouse was making clutch bags for Jean Muir, and Lesley Slight's appliquéd leather envelope bags in fashionable pale shades were widely admired. Belts and clutch bags in suede and leather came from Gucci, the company's slim, suede envelope bags sealed with a golden "G," and other leading names from Ferragamo to Saint Laurent Rive Gauche and Condotti, put forward their own clutches. For the younger generation, supple leather bags decorated with Japanese batik were available from Ito, on Second Avenue, New York.

Simple, chic, and expensive, this Gucci clutch bag is made in the finest black leather, and supported by a substantial metal frame.

A red "wet look" leather shoulder bag is shaped and padded and has an external pocket closing with a fish-shaped silver clasp. Italian made by Fior in 1973.

From 1975, clutches began to be called purses in Britain, and tended to be rather more workman-like than those made in America or Continental Europe. Typical were the tan and leather, quilted clutch bags from Mulberry, while synthetics were employed to make bags such as the 1976 bright red, nylon cire pochette by Trimfit.

Purses to Wear with the Layered Look

It was designers such as Kenzo, under the label of Jap, who introduced the layered look of the mid-1970s. Longer, flared skirt lengths were worn with layered woollens, capes, scarves, knitted hats, decorative pantihose, and squashy boots in an orgy of color and pattern. Large, knitted or crocheted bags were worn diagonally across the body, as were patchwork, cotton shoulder purses or pockets which fastened with a little button from Jap & Joseph. Emerald and violet, satin shoulder purses with brilliant embroideries accompanied skull caps, Chinese waistcoats, and trousers.

Pouch purses in suede and leather slung over one shoulder were worn inside a coat, and Sonia Rykiel introduced her hip and leather purses on belts. Small, leather shoulder bags from Charles Jourdan in 1976 and flat, tan leather purses with pockets, to be worn around the neck, were both in keeping with their time.

Satchels too suited the layered styles of the day. Their functional air of innocence ensured their popularity, and they were made in green canvas and tan leather by Jap, in Indian red/brown leather by Christopher Trill from London store Joseph, and in cream canvas by Upla for casual day wear, also available from Joseph. Jump suits and wedge-heeled espadrilles were teamed up with a red satchel by Trimfit in 1976, while quilted, sand, canvas and sepia leather satchels were sold by Feathers.

The Big, Soft Shoulder Bag

The casual, layered look, with minimal accessories and accompanied by a large, soft leather shoulder bag in natural tones, was epitomized by the model Lauren Hutton, the face of the 1970s. Women were striving for a clean, natural look with fluid clothes in shades of beige and neutrals. There was a preference for natural fabrics and real leather accessories, with shoes, boots, shoulder bags, and briefcases made in soft tan, brown, and burgundy calf leather.

One of the reasons that the soft shoulder bag was so successful was that increasingly large numbers of working women needed a portable lifestyle bag that was both relaxed and functional. It had to age gracefully, but still look good despite being thrown on the floor. Women demanded more of their clothes—expecting them to be machine washable, hard-wearing, and flexible—and more from their bags.

The soft leather shoulder bag that had evolved from the ethnic look of the late 1960s became a stylish, capacious, and flexible accessory that was helpful to women, rather than being a responsibility. It became the dominant handbag style of the late 1970s, summed up by Loewe's casual, although expensive, printed suede totes and those from the Italian-based firm, Enny, whose 'softbags' had been selling since 1966. Covered in external pockets, these bags were quite different from the country shoulder bag, and were infinitely urban, if not suburban. The look became glamorized when large, soft, gold leather shoulder bags by Barbara Bolan were featured in American *Vogue* in 1977.

Shoulder bags appeared in any number of styles, from a blue leather one by Charles Jourdan to huge printed suede tote bags with knotted straps and zippered tops by Loewe. The

les must de *Cartier*
Paris

In spite of the fact that the decade was dominated by young fashion, traditional bagmakers continued to find a market for well made, classic bags.

A soft leather shoulder bag became a necessary item in a busy woman's life. This silver-colored leather bag was spacious and practical, in spite of its glamorous appearance.

Purple felt fun "flower power" bag in a squashy flower shape, zip fastening, and fabric wrist handle.

A shoulder bag in red velour stripes, with black leather trim and handles was made by Aldana for Fior, Italy in 1970. Aldana also made bags for Gucci.

Dick Whittington bag was designed to be worn with blanket jackets, big watches, scarves, and felt hats, while matched riding boots and polished leather double shoulder purses in the softest leather were also made by Loewe. Huge shoulder bags were teamed up with trousers, collarless shirts and blazers with big lapels, as seen on display in Woody Allen's film *Annie Hall* of 1971. Diane Keaton, the leading lady, was costumed by Ralph Lauren in feminine versions of men's wear, sporting tortoiseshell glasses, oversized shirts, hacking jackets, fedoras, and large shoulder bags. The film inspired a host of lookalikes in both America and Europe.

Swimming Against the Tide

In contrast to the masculine look, a new romanticism emerged around 1974 which derived from the summer look of the 1930s. The resulting bias cut dresses were made in crêpe and jersey, many exploiting the brilliant primary colors that were popular in the early 1970s. Merged with the 1930s look was a delight in antique clothes, with lace petticoats worn deliberately below the hemline of a dress.

To accompany such frills and flounces, antique bags began to be very collectable. Clutch bags in authentic 1930s style were made by the likes of Christopher Trill, who created rose leather purses with stripes of snakeskin, and substantial flap front clutch bags in ginger and cream stripes, and Condotti. Their clutches were made from natural and black woven straw.

There was a vogue for flowered dresses and smocks, with full-length, Liberty print flowered smocks on sale at Harrods with matching flowered handbags. Their maker, Brigid Martineau, reintroduced the wrist strap to get around the problem of holding the clutch bag. The country rose look of straw hats and flowered dresses was reflected in leather purses flowered in shades of rose and cream, some of the best made by the talented British designer, Clive Shilton. His raffia purses, eau de nil leather purses with quilted flower sides, and quilted, scallop shell bags of 1976 were all acclaimed.

Country Bags for City Slickers

One reason behind the success of Roger Saul's Mulberry company was its products chimed perfectly with the 1970s quest of the town dweller for the healthy outdoors. Big fishing and hunting satchels, were made by many companies, including a large khaki, canvas fishing bag by Whistles in 1977, and were snapped up by urban working women in town. Such large, countrified shoulder bags gave the impression that women had the option of being urban or rural, the freedom to drop everything at a moment's notice for an invitation to the country.

In the aspiring Britain of the 1970s, this pre-occupation with 'country' was a hang-over from the aristocratic social season, much of which took place in the country. The nation was swept with a wave of conservatism, and was shortly to vote Magaret Thatcher's Conservative Party into power in 1979. In the USA, similar conservative sentiment elected President Reagan to the White House, and was evident in a similar attachment to country bags.

Until then, country bags had followed the same pattern for decades. One American designer, Anne Fogarty, expressed her opinion on bag fashions for the country in the magazine *Wife Dressing*. "A small, ineffectual bag with heavy tweeds is just silly," she wrote. "You need a large rugged handbag to round off the ensemble." Country handbags were never cheap, because of their high quality, but they broadened the definition and style of casual, country-inspired wear enormously. They became high fashion statements in the 1970s, and also hinted at social mobility, the rise of the individual entrepreneur, and the aspirations of the working woman.

Among the most noted makers of such bags were Dooney & Bourke of Connecticut, USA, established in 1975 by H. Peter Dooney and Frederick Bourke. Peter Dooney began working in leather in his teens, and his designs—many of which are influenced by equestrian leather fittings—continue to define the company's products today. Like the Mulberry Company, traditionalism and craftsmanship were the mainstay of Dooney & Bourke's philosophy. Both shared a pride in the leather work traditions of their respective countries, while allying this to a modernity of design application for contemporary living. Dooney & Bourke's trademark "All Weather Leather," a naturally shrunken, waterproof cowhide with a pebbly texture which the company reintroduced, ensured that their bags improved with age.

In Britain, one town adaptation of the country look appeared in the form of sleeveless, quilted jackets, shirts, and skirts, worn with head scarves tied on the chin and an expensive looking, leather shoulder handbag. This simple way of "dressing down", worn by the wealthy, took off in America as the "preppie" look, and later became popular in Japan. The tote and the casual shoulder bag were the perfect accompaniment for such outfits, and were often bought through mail order catalogs such as L. L. Bean's.

Patent, leather Fior bag with an overall floral pattern of white on black. It has a matching shoulder strap and hexagonal silver clasp.

So what's in your handbag?

Larger handbags meant more room to be filled, and prompted a growing list of high-status consumer goods on sale to high flyers. British *Vogue* suggested in November 1976 that those fearful of dropping their handbags and being shown up by its contents should consider stocking it with stylish accessories. Its suggestions? A "9ct gold key-ring that's a key itself, a big money clip in gold for your gold, ribbed, gold-plated Moulure lighter, all from Cartier. Solid black Mont Blanc fountain pen from Asprey. Bagsize address book for London, Paris, and New York. Black memo card holder with gold corners…the Pulsar watch that's a digital clock on a chain…the spy's camera, an Olympus" … and that's just to start with.

CASHING IN ON THE GLOBAL ECONOMY

As handbags had international application, and were less liable to instant fashion changes and whims, bags were easy to export. Nor were there problems with sizing, as in shoes. Many handbag manufacturers sold their goods worldwide, with outlets in all the major cities. Many American companies exported handbags, but the country was a massive importer of stylish goods from Italy and France, despite the success of their own indigenous designers and makers. La Bagagerie, from Paris, sold their relaxed bags and chic Madras leather clutches in their Madison Avenue branch (they had another in Tokyo) while Italians Roberta di Camerino sold their characteristic, ornate handbags with trademark embossed logo in outlets all over the USA. Top French designers such as Jeanne Lanvin had been established in America for years—her store on the Avenue of the Americas sold stylish bags for mature women—and many others opened boutiques selling accessories and cheaper lines around the country.

The Cult of the Logo

Visible labels, designer "signatures," and trademark logos began to appear on everything from jeans to sunglasses in the 1970s. The consumer's increased independence impelled designers to develop attention-grabbing tactics to publicize their names, and the late 1960s disenchantment with designer fashions made this all the more necessary. Status dressing and the conspicuous display of designer objects became almost a cult, and the handbag was no exception.

Handbags, being physically independent of their owner in a way that shoes and hats are not, presented the perfect vehicles for advertising. The paper carrier bag from certain revered stores already had cachet, and now, the previously anonymous handbag could demand equal billing.

A taupe, patent leather day bag made by Lewis, its double straps continue around the boxy shape, somewhat in imitation of travel bag styles.

These classic bags (*above*) were made in all types of leather for more than ten years, between 1966 and 1976 by Jane Shilton.

A small, red leather Fior bag, with a leather handle, brass trimmings, and fine precision made clasp, made in Italy in 1976.

In 1970, Gucci's leather, zipper topped shoulder bags adopted the "G" already worn around the neck on Gucci chains. The initial itself was used as an adornment. The same idea was picked up in 1972 by Christian Dior, when his identifying initials were turned into a decorative pattern for the company's huge, brown and white printed fabric and leather carrier with overarm straps. Saint Laurent Rive Gauche's capacious, beige-printed canvas and brown leather shoulder bags followed suit, as did bags from Jaeger.

Dressing for Evening

At the end of the 1960s, the ostentatious costume jewelry that had been all the rage was rejected. It was thought better to wear little or no jewelry at all than to wear fakes, and the minimalist gold chain came into vogue, some invisibly thin, others more substantial. Evening bags, always influenced by jewelry fashions, also became simpler, although still luxurious. Affluent bag buyers invested in Oroton's mesh bags with a metal snake strap, or Halston's black satin envelopes of 1972.

By the mid 1970s, evening bags reflected the new softness and romanticism seen in clothes of muted colors. White satin, double pleated evening bags were created by the British craftsman Clive Shilton, worn with skimpy, knee-length dresses in clingy rayon jersey, and he also made shell bags in screenprinted satin and soft leather. An alternative to pale colors were found in dramatic evening bags of black and metallics. Harvey Nichols sold envelopes of "golden scales," while Charles Jourdan's black suede envelope bags on a strap of black and diamante, from 1977, were meant to be worn with a black suit and gold kid cummerbund. Christopher Trill's tiny, silver kid duffel bag was a hit in 1976, and Lisandro Sarasola produced a lamé leopard bag.

A series of shoulder bags in an evening version of the little shoulder pouch were made by Cartier in 1979. These were embellished with "blooms of marguerites, bouquets of roses centered with jet or seed pearls, topaz, and other semi-precious stones; gold thread delicately embroidered onto suede." Each bag was accompanied by a matching suede neck tie, clipped with a twist of gold. Cartier described them as a "new way of wearing jewelry: an intriguing mix of the finest silks, suede, gold, and jewels creating a fashion masterpiece." Picking up the idea of replacing the necklace completely, Bill Gibb's gilded and padded fan pockets piped with gold were designed to be worn around the neck.

Holding on to Tradition

Those who did not want to excite controversy provided a loyal following for the traditional handbag, and more old-fashioned, structured styles continued to be made

Paco Rabanne-inspired bag with small, gold and silver-colored metal discs over gold fabric, has a link chain and a metal clasp closing, was made in Italy during the 1970s.

for formal occasions such as weddings and christenings. Women who wished to, which often included those in the public eye, were still able to purchase a classic bag from the many companies who prided themselves on being independent of fashion. Britain's Launer, handbag manufacturer to the Queen, was among them.

Several companies updated the classics, from Britain's Hardy Amies, whose maroon leather handbag was featured with a tweedy trouser suit in 1972, to French designer Etienne Aigner, who made briefcases, half circle shoulder purses, and other structured bags. Robinson's of Southern California produced "Spanish spectators" handbags in patent and suede with brass trimmings, and Buti specialized in Italian handbags.

By the mid 1970s, the economic recession in Europe and the United States had lead to leather shortages. Handbag prices went up, and what had once been the cornerstone of a woman's wardrobe became a luxury item. Many young women grew up never having owned a "good" bag, and thought it quite normal to go without, although they were spoilt for choice when it came to bags that reflected the fashions of the day.

Small, turquoise velour shoulder bag with black embroidery and flap front trimmed with a deep gold fringe and gold tassle on the strap. Made in Italy by Cesare Ficcini, and designed by Charles Jourdan.

Translatlantic skill sharing

Among the oldest and most successful of upmarket American bag manufacturers is Mark Cross. The company was famously featured in Alfred Hitchcock's film *Rear Window* of 1954 (Grace Kelly tucks her negligée and slippers into a small, top-handled Cross handbag,) but although the publicity made a good story, the company had already been established for many years. It was set up by Henry W. Cross, an Irish saddler who served his apprenticeship in London and then emigrated to the United States in 1845. He soon established a company of harness and trunk makers in Boston, in which his son Mark later served an apprenticeship. Mark was then sent back to a traditional leather-working center in Walsall, England, to study leather craftsmanship, before returning to America with his specialist knowledge. He went on to set up the bag manufacturers that continues to produce quality bags to this day. The firm is now owned by Sarah Lee, but it continues to specialize in traditional English techniques for working hide and leather.

"Epic Ski" holdall by Karrimor.

The Triumph of the Sportsbag

In the 1970s, when the ideal woman's figure was slim, willowy, and natural, fitness became a sport of its own, rather than the preliminary training for sportsmen and women that it had always been.

Adidas' high profile logo into has become a sporty fashion statement (*above*).

Celebrities and famous actresses brought fitness into the home by producing exercise videos, and sportswear departments took over from the old millinery and couture departments of stores as they closed down, their day gone. The craze for skateboarding filled every street corner, with its young exponents honing both their skills and their fashions in equal measure.

The fitness explosion was paralleled by the marketing of named accessories, including sports bags, by companies such as Nike, Adidas, Puma, Fila, and Champion. The leotard look became absorbed into mainstream fashion with the development of Lycra exercise clothes, and the many health clubs and dance studios which sprang up opened their own small sports fashion outlets. They supplied Lycra leotards, exercise tights, special shoes, and head bands, and also offered were the nylon bags with which to carry it all. Sports bags soon became status symbols in their Day-glo nylon or disguised as a leather briefcase, and were prized equally by men and women. Certain bags became as covetable as a Chanel "2.55" quilted handbag

It's All in the Name

Garments and accessories which were once worn exclusively by sports men and women became affordable and available, and before long, running shoes were seen everwhere. As their popularity grew, a lucrative business in bootlegging logos and brand names sprang up. As often as not, running shoes were worn with shell suits in bright colors, based on original designs for sportswear, and sausage-shaped shoulder bags by Reebok, most of which were made in Taiwan.

Every park seemed to have its share of joggers in tracksuits, their essentials secured in waist bags or tiny shoulder bags worn diagonally across the body. Roller discos became the latest vogue, the shiny bright

Paul Smith
BAG

MANUFACTURED AND DISTRIBUTED BY YOSHINAGA CORPORATION
INFORMATION: PAUL SMITH JAPAN 03-3486 1500

AD:ABOUD PHOTOGRAPHY:Y.SODANO

Paul Smith took the square style and structure of a record bag (*left*), added some sporty colors, and create a more general-purpose holdall.

Fun rucksacks like the Adidas example (*below*) took the place of traditional leather school bags.

colors of Lycra oufits and matching bags reflecting the poundingly loud music, while cycling fashions brought tight Elastane shorts and the "bum bag" into mainstream fashion.

On the Beach

Among the couture designers, American Perry Ellis introduced his sportswear label in 1978 and Giorgio di Sant' Angelo's fascination with stretchy workout fabrics resulted in body suits in wild colors. One beach wardrobe in white matte stretch fabric had a bikini, wrap top, and tie skirt all folding into a small matching bag.

The small lightweight bag reached its heights in the 1980s with Le Sportsac, a vast range of bags made by the American company of the same name. Colorful drawstring duffels, biking or skiing waist bags, bags for workouts, for weekending, for the office, portfolios, totes, and handbags were sewn from specially coated parachute nylon, bound with tough carpet tape, and strapped with webbing. They weighed as little as 15 oz (420g) but could carry up to 40 lbs (36 kg), and always came in a little zipped pouch with the company name on it. They sold all over the world.

Sports accessories have been characterized by both their practicality and their fashionability, and bags were no exception, emblazoned with the maker's label or logo. By the last years of the 20th century, the sportswear revolution had been embraced by young people everywhere, and sports bags had become part of popular street style, from ghettos to shopping malls. Transparent swimming bags, squash bags, golf bags by Mulberry, mini-sports rucksacks, and huge nylon totes generated by the fitness explosion were all destined to become part of the cultural heritage of fashionable accessories.

Fake mother-of-pearl plastic disk-shaped bag (*right*) typical of Biba's innovative 70s style,

The Biba Phenomenon

In the mid 1970s, a retailing phenomenon hit the London fashion scene. It drew on 20s and 30s decadence for inspiration, added a multitude of new colors, and made striking style affordable for the ordinary person.

Polish-born Barbara Hulanicki started to make her name by winning beachwear design competition run by a leading London newspaper. She then became a fashion illustrator, and in 1963, set up Biba's Postal Boutique, a fashion mail order business named after her younger sister. The first Biba boutique opened in London a year later, and moved to the fashionable Kensington district soon afterwards.

Before long, Biba's success was assured by the steady stream of celebrities who poured through its doors. Television personality Cathy McGowan, hostess of the pop music show *Ready, Steady, Go*, pop singer Cilla Black, actress Julie Christie, model Twiggy, and musicians from Sonny and Cher to Mick Jagger, all became dedicated customers.

In 1970, Hulanicki established a satellite Biba boutique at the Bergdorf Goodman flagship store in New York. A special window display summed up the Biba look, the dresses draped on dark bentwood hat stands, matching hats and bags...a model of a vampish, 1930s siren with dark make-up, spotted net veil, and canvas, knee-length, side-zipped boots. The ornate Art Nouveau Biba logo in black and gold was seen everywhere, and there were tall totes made from canvas dyed in vibrant shades, and boots in every imaginable color.

Affordable Style

Biba's appeal was that it was totally unique. Communal changing rooms were introduced, and among the dimly lit clothes displays were potted plants and a myriad accessories. The place overflowed with feather boas, Lurex pantyhose, beads, and scoop-neck vests in every possible color. Many colors were from the "granny" palette of dark plum and black, and were even found in lipsticks. Finishing touches were added with bags and snakeskin belts from Roger Saul, the founder of Mulberry, when he was still making them on his kitchen table.

From dresses to jewelry, cosmetics, and underwear, the Biba look struck a chord in a new generation of British girls to whom French couture was remote and irrelevant. Even more important, the store's prices were totally affordable—as Hulanicki said, "We practically gave our things away to the public."

In common with the look of the time, the first Biba bags were small shoulder bags in quilted leather, their narrow chain straps threaded through large eyelets. They were made in mock crocodile, leather, and plastic of all colors, and were meant to be worn with, and often matched the short, simple, mini-dresses that were another Hulanicki trademark.

In June 1965, "the floweriest fashion scene for many a summer," Biba was described in British *Vogue*, and included a Biba flower-printed bra and zipper-topped handbag covered in "fantasy flowers scattered lightly on shady blond linen." These were teamed with an enamel sunflower ring by Corocraft, giant bloom earrings by Adrien Mann, and flowered linen shoes by Bally. As Biba's styles became more influenced by the 1930s, languid, decadent models with heavily made-up eyes were pictured in satin dresses and hats with spotted veils. Clutch bags featured more, a spotted clutch accompanying a satin mini-wrap over a dress and huge hat, for example. More structured leather and metal handbags appeared in the 1970s, teamed with wide trousers, known as "bags", faded cardigans in marled wool, and lace-up shoes.

By 1969, 100,000 shoppers a week were passing through the Biba boutiques; they were on the tourist map of London, and designers scoured the store for fresh ideas. In 1973, Hulanicki took over the failing department store of Derry & Toms in Kensington, an enormous 1930s building and launched Big Biba. But before long, the extravaganza collapsed and eventually went bankrupt in 1976, beset by financial and family problems.

"Rogers" briefcase showing
solid brass fittings and the
Mulberry leather tag.

The Rise of the Mulberry Company

The founder of what is now a multil-national corporation, with its biggest market in America, started his business on the kitchen table of his London flat.

"Tsarina" bag in mock crocodile leather.

Roger Saul formed Mulberry in 1969, making snakeskin leather chokers and belts on the kitchen table of his London flat, which he sold to Biba and other famous London boutiques. He is now head of a national corporation with 52 retail outlets around the world.

By 1971, Saul had set up the Mulberry label and launched its first collection of bags and belts. Four years later, Mulberry bags were seen in *Vogue* magazine, teamed with fur jackets, and knitted wool hats. By 1976, the signature range of Mulberry leather accessories was in production. Created for both men and women, it was inspired by the clothes worn for outdoor country pursuits.

Mulberry's conservative but stylish shoulder bags, briefcases, and wallets are crafted and finished with great care, in keeping with Roger Saul's driving passion for beautifully made and finished products. Solid brass fittings and an embossed Mulberry bush logo appear on all the products. Materials included drummed leather, crocodile, and alligator skin, embossed leather, and smooth calf. The synthetic, hardwearing Scotchgrain, with its polyvinyl outer layer and embossed pebble grain finish, was introduced in 1984. Typical designs in the early 1970s included big shoulder bags in beige, quilted fabric, bound with dark leather, and suede pigskin, canvas, and net "fishing bags".

As early as 1977, America became Mulberry's biggest market, and a concessionary store was opened in the upscale store Nieman-Marcus. Despite the U.S. stock market crash and world recession in 1980, Mulberry went from strength to strength, expanding into shoe collections, franchise shops, toiletries, home collections, watches, fragrance, sportswear, and ready-to-wear collections. Nonetheless, it is for its leather accessories that Mulberry remains best known.

Keeping Pace with the Rising Tide of Consumerism

As the economies of Europe and America spiraled upwards, higher wages and standards of living led to a huge increase in consumerism. Designer names and logos became ever more important status symbols, appearing on clothes, bags, and other accessories as well as more unexpected goods such as chocolates and mineral water. Acquiring a lifestyle by owning a recognizable label was the aim of the day, and such displays of financial success flooded the media and shopping malls alike. Designer labels were no longer the prerogative of the super rich, and although named bags were generally conservative classics in the early 1980s, they soon embraced the exaggerated styles of the mid decade. The prosperity of the 1980s manifested itself in ostentatious glamor, epitomized by such television shows as the oil rich, Dallas-based soap opera *Dynasty*. As the decade progressed, fashion had a certainty that it lacked in the early years, and by the mid 1980s, exaggeration was the key. Bold jewelry with chunky chains and large semi-precious stones was worn with big hats and patterned fabrics. At last there seemed something to party for, and evening wear and accessories became ever more dramatic.

The Princess of Wales (*above*) poses with Danielle Mitterand, wife of the former French President—the princess is carrying a light-blue, silk clutch bag. Mock croc evening bag (*right*) in a simple, elegant style.

DESIGNER DOLLARS

In America, the strength of the US dollar fueled the desire for European handbags and accessories, and the Hermes scarf and Kelly bag, the Chanel quilted gilt chained bag, and Gucci bamboo handled bags became small, expensive statements of wealth. As the years passed, the scale and color of handbags reflected the new confidence in dressing, and quiet, polished leather bags in natural shades of brown and russet were replaced by the fashion conscious by reptile skin bags in electric shades. The professional woman carried bold black bags inspired by men's briefcases or baggage.

Fashion designers recognized the new significance of accessories, and expanded their collections to include hats, shoes and bags. In 1985, for example, American designer Liz Claiborne purchased the accessory firm of Kaiser-Roth Corporation, the company she had previously licensed to manufacture her handbags. Clothes became less formal, and accessories took over the role of dramatizing an outfit, providing accents of color, contrast and style.

Total looks in fashion were provided by American designers such as Donna Karan, who displayed her clothes and accessories together in her stores, both to help busy women dress themselves elegantly, and also to promote her concepts. In 1988, she launched the DKNY branches, which sold her less expensive range of clothes and accessories. Fellow designers Ralph Lauren, Anne Klein, Adrienne Vittadini, Calvin Klein, and Geoffrey Beene also provided complete outfits, including bags and shoes.

In Europe too, fashion houses saw the growing significance of accessories and launched advertising campaigns to promote their hats and handbags. Designers Cardin, Armani, Alaïa, Claude Montana, Versace, Lacroix, Chanel, Galliano, and Ozbeck ruled supreme, while specialist accessory stores proliferated on both sides of the Atlantic, from Mario of Florence to Susan Bennis/Warren Edwards and Helene Arpels of New York.

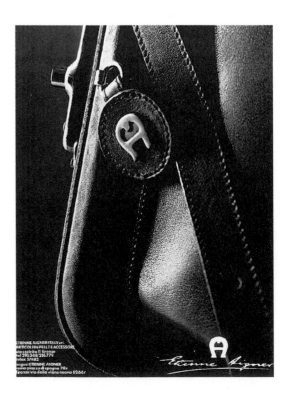

1980s, stylish, two-tone bag (*top*) in white and black leather with topstitching and flap closing, with short handle, made by Magli, Italy. White, quilted leather vanity-style bag (*bottom*) with zip opening, made in Italy in the 1980s by Magli, a footwear company which has recently diversified into handbags.

Long-handled, leather handbag (*right*). The stitching and metal buckles emphasize the texture and style of this bag made by Etienne Aigner in Italy.

Opening with Decorum

The early 1980s were distinguished by a taste for sober, quiet handbags. Christopher Trill's soft suede shoulder bag with its zipper top, in shades such as ash grey, was typical, as were Etienne Aigner's burgundy leather drawstring shoulder bags.

The Italians continued to play a major role in exporting bags, and the company "i santi" sold its diva line of framed, pouchy handbags from branches in Europe and the USA. Another Italian leather company, Enny, built on their success of the late 1970s with distinctive shoulder bags and totes, including kidney-shaped, mushroom leather shoulder bags in 1980, stamped, chocolate patent leather shoulder bags, and gray, double-pocketed shoulder bags with zippered tops.

All in One Bag

For many women, Enny provided the answer to carrying everything needed for a busy day, but with style. A new range of bags made of rubberized cotton, and with French calf leather straps, was introduced in the early 1980s, made in the Enny factory outside Florence. These were styled like any leather bag but were lightweight, water repellent, and always able to stretch enough to accommodate one thing more. They were sturdy, trimmed in leather, had lots of pockets, so that everything was organized, and were made in irresistible jelly bean colors.

The possibilities of lightweight, supple plastics were also explored by Jerry and Morris Moskowitz, brothers who had run the American company of Morris Moskowitz for over thirty years. They combined plastic with leather, typically weaving together one matte and one patent strand to make their bags and belts. The strands were often in contrasting colors, as seen on a clutch bag in black patent and red matte leather in 1980, and on a black patent and yellow leather tote of the same year.

The old established company of Whiting & Davis, known in their heyday in the 1920s and 1930s for their evening mesh bags, continued to produce their speciality. In the early 1980s, they reworked their mesh into daytime, leather-lined, mesh

Elegant, hand-crafted saddle bag (*left*) made of brown crocodile and lustred calf and designed by Joan and David to produce a simple shape with rounded base and flap.

A geometric, patterned envelope bag (*right*) produced from a patchwork of ostrich, alligator and calf in red, white and black. Possibly inspired by Russian revolutionary abstract art such as that produced by Malevich in the late teens and early 1920s.

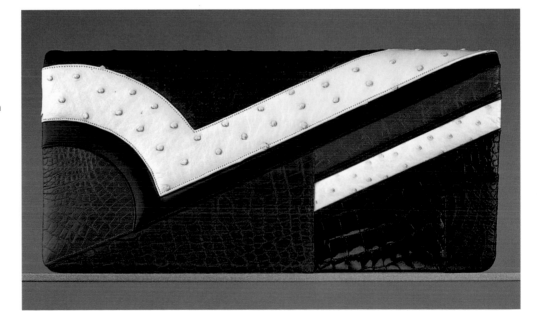

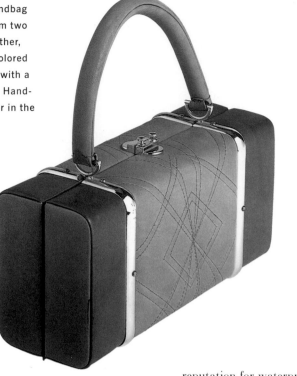

Suitcase-shaped handbag (*right*) produced from two shades of brown leather, bound with a gold colored metal trim and lock with a single, rigid handle. Hand-made in Italy for Fior in the 1980s.

portfolios, mesh mufflers with ombre edging, and saddle shoulder bags in plated and often printed mesh.

Casual but Elegant

Even saddlery-influenced casual and country bags took on a new sophistication in the 1980s. La Bagagerie made small shoulder bags in pony skin with leather trim—others were dyed bright colors—and Hunting World produced a sporty, dark brown leather shoulder bag with bridle leather trim. Handsome hunting bags in warm natural leather were created by B. Altman.

As always, the most exclusive ranges used only the best quality materials. Investment classics such as shoulder bags on shoestring, slim straps from Nazareno Gabrielli were made in luxurious, soft napa leather, with soft curving lines. The most sought after of lines from the top designers included Ralph Lauren's Polo collection, which featured the Karabu saddlebag, and the "Club Check" shoulder bag with leather trim from the British firm, Aquascutum.

Burberry, another traditional British company, which carried the Royal warrant "By Appt to Her Majesty The Queen and Queen Mother" as Weather Proofers. Their long-held reputation for waterproof coats and accessories enjoyed a boost in the mid 1980s when "the Burberry look" was especially popular with the French and the Japanese.

Old European companies such as Goldpfeil, established in 1856 and which made handcrafted leather goods from Bavarian hides in their Offenbach factories in Western Germany, made a feature of their longevity. Classic bags with the cachet of history took precedence over overtly modern examples in the convention led 1980s, and even firms with no history self consciously invented one with advertising campaigns and nostalgic packaging.

Appreciating age

A growing fascination with antiques and collectibles grabbed the 1980s consumer, and television shows on the subject were watched by millions. At home, nostalgic versions of countrified room settings were created by interior decorators, with floral patterns and scrubbed wooden furniture.

Those with an eye to an investment in the handbag world looked to purchase early bags, such as vanity cases from the 1920s and beaded bags. Prices rose for collectors' items, with one 18K yellow gold antique purse sold for $15,000 at Cartier's in 1981. It had special compartments for powder, lipstick, lip gloss, and perfume.

Two shoulder bags and zip-up make-up bag (*below*) by minimalist Jill Sander, in warm beige and putty colored leather using muted colors to produce a soft, simple, functional style.

A 1980s, Joan and David waist bag (*below*) attached to a brown, leather belt and designed with a leather trim and white topstitching to produce a practical yet attractive country/explorer look.

A typical 1980s shoulder bag (*above*), designed by Fior and made of soft, white, patent leather with a front flap which has an exaggerated tab and circular, gold-colored metal trim.

Picking up the color

Confident, off-beat tones of magenta, raspberry, and turquoise became popular in the early 1980s, worked into equally bold, geometric patterning. A persimmon red, hexagonal shoulder bag in bamboo was presented by Rafael Sanchez Designs Limited (USA), and quilted leather shoulder bags, striped and strapped in bold bi-colors, came from the workshops of American Jerry Kott. The French design house Chloé, fronted by designer Karl Lagerfeld, offered a red plastic fish shoulder bag on a long, red shoulder strap, and half-circular, leather shoulder bags in bright colors were made by Charles Jourdan. Mulberry launched a range of half moon bags.

For the young and/or wacky, Malcolm Parsons made coppered and brown, cardboard clutch bags which only cost a few dollars, finished off with dark red, enamel trim, while the Italian company Fiorucci sold inexpensive shocking pink plastic shoulder bags in their stores worldwide. Brightly spotted, plastic envelope bags were available all over Britain from Jump Accessories.

Equipped for a Career

Fashion styles for the career woman in the 1980s included suits and ensembles with masculine tailoring. Specific stores opened in America to cater specifically for the business woman, supplying wide-shouldered trouser suits and jackets that were perfect for taking the weight of a large shoulder bag.

Dressing for success meant having handbags with integral personal organizers, calculators, and calendars, while women were also encouraged to carry flashlights, whistles, and tins of mace to use for self protection. Briefcases became more elegant and feminine, with examples such as the "Trafalgar," a soft brown leather and brass-buckled briefcase by Marley Hodgson, or the Karabu portfolio by Polo/Ralph Lauren for more formal work situations. For the super ambitious, Gucci made a briefcase in Bordeaux lizard which sold at $2300.

The new generation of working bags provided combinations that would cover every need. US *Vogue* suggested that women should carry one small bag in an unusual color or different texture, such as a small shaped clutch or its equivalent, for wallet, keys, and small personal items, and a second bag for working essentials. This would encompass everything else that women had to carry in the 1980s, from paperwork to spare shoes and a low calorie lunch. A wide range of

A novelty shoulder bag (*right*) of the 1980s, designed by Marilyn Brooks, containing a clock face with Roman numerals set into black plastic. It was made in Taiwan and imported by Liberty.

Systematic bag carrying

By 1988, women were finding their totes becoming so full and weighty that a new solution had to be found. Donna Karan was one—her driver had to deliver her tote to work while she walked—and she, among others, devised "systems" for working women which increased the number of their bags to three or four. A small evening bag was carried in a tote, while a leather knapsack worn on the back held a shoulder bag for going out to lunch and daytime use.

Maria Manetti Farrow, designer of the new Mark Cross Leather Goods Collection, had two favorite systems. One was a large tote containing two 'organized' nylon zip pouches, while another held a narrow attaché and a medium-sized shoulder bag. Others, such as jewelry designer Carole Rochas, simply pared down the number of bags required. Rochas possessed a leather Pellegrino bag in every classic color, each of which contained an inside zipper pocket to carry samples to clients, a simple cosmetic bag, and a post-it pad to make notes on.

totes, carryalls, and portfolios in interesting colors and textures developed to fulfil these needs.

Bags for All Occasions

There was Bagheera's wine leather drawstring saddlebag, Fendi's flat, snap-front tote in sage green embossed leather, and multi pocketed, rubberized, purple bags by Enny, as well as their huge, pepper red carryall with matching smaller bag. Bottega Veneta's bright red, city tote was especially roomy, and a little more dressy, while Mark Cross made bucket totes in embossed, camel colored leather. Ralph Lauren/Polo made casual totes, Louis Vuitton made weekend totes, and B. Altman & Co, totes in warm natural leathers.

Good looking, well thought-out bags designed to work were considered essential, and most practical of all was to carry two at a time. Enormous weekend bags with flap fronted pockets, shoulder strap, and handles, made by Enny in 1986, were meant to be worn with matching shoulder bag, while many women owned a fashionable sports bag, such as those made by the American company LeSportsac. Having earned their money, working women turned their attention to their physique, and keeping fit became a new obsession.

A Louis Vuitton shoulder bag (*above*) made of monogrammed printed canvas with leather trim. Strap extends around sides and buckle around exterior, fastening at the flap front.

A WONDERFUL VARIETY

In the early 1980s, there were cherry red, textured leather clutches from Coach Leatherware and small, dark brown, pressed leather shoulder bags with a shiny, waterproof coating from Enny. Most handbags were small with a shoulder strap, such as the small, crisp, clean white shoulder bags sharpened with red – all with signature vanity mirror – produced by the international American handbag designer Lou Taylor Handbags. Hunting World, on the other hand, made roomy, countrified, leather-trimmed envelopes.

Textured and embossed Valentino bags were sold in Paris in drawstring cotton bags complete with the V logo, alongside neat Etienne Aigner bags. Also in Paris, La Bagagerie featured small, neat shoulder bags in chic two-tones and little shoulder bags knotted at the front, designed by Jean Marlaix in different colors, in their 1985 spring/summer collection. Verlaine's handbags were ornately topstitched, Yves St Laurent had a hit with hats, belts, bags, and gloves, and François Marot produced satchel-like bags in cream and tan. Lancel's patterned canvas with their L logo and stitched leather label appeared on shoulder bags, wallets, weekend bags, and duffels drawn to with silk cord.

Nearing the middle of the decade, American Harpers *Bazaar* declared that "Nothing does more for an outfit than the right

The Umbrella Bag (*above*) is part of a collection by Jane Shilton called organizers with unzipped pocket for matching umbrella.

This 1980s outfit (*above*) features a floral suit, heart bracelet and, as the finishing touch, a richly patterned silk clutch bag. Designed by Yves Saint Laurent, it provides a rich tapestry of color and sparkle.

With publicity campaigns as inventive and striking as their products, Moschino presented this important-looking leather bag (*above*) with "baroque"-shaped, gilt metal handle on an ornate carved table.

accessory—in neutral colors, natural materials. Must-haves for any working woman's starting-out wardrobe: one classic watch, subtle jewelry, a luggage leather belt and one richly toned bag." Examples abounded, from lambskin saddlebags with brown kidskin trim by La Bagagerie to tan, woven leather clutches with optional shoulder strap by Bottega Veneta. Carlos Falchi produced both brick, waterbuffalo leather slouch totes with double shoulder straps and white, water buffalo leather portfolios with shoulder straps. Cognac leather duffels by Gianello came from Barneys of New York.

Finding the Right Bag for Night

Evening bags such as the silvered straw and black silk, tasseled bags from Rafael Sanchez, on sale at Joseph in London, were typical designs of the early 1980s. But by the mid 1980s, the evening bag styles that remained were either feminine, as in the 1985 Neri bags from Grant of Knightsbridge with tulip and flower leather appliqué shapes, or glamorous, typified by the 1986 evening bags of Judith Teller, whose quality leather handbags and accessories included pleated silk evening clutch bags with geometric frames. Equally glamorous were jewel encrusted eggs by James

White, leather, matching vanity-style bag and shoes (*above*) with glitzy, silver flecks adding that glamorous, 1980s disco look.

Shoulder tote, brown mock croc leather, simple bag (*below*) with thin straps continuing around its exterior. Designed by Joan and David.

1980s trend towards fur, glitz and glamor—Fendi was the ultimate fashion statement in the 80s with its "F" logo on the outside of bags and accessories.

Arpad, sophisticated blue and orange paillettes on leather with chain straps by Jill Stuart, and quilted, beaded, purple satin bags by Barbara Bolan Too.

In the second half of the decade, a new exoticism crept in—Indian-jeweled and gold-embroidered, black velvet evening bags were seen about town, as was the dramatic new Black Zucca fabric, unique to Fendi. Introduced in 1988 and printed with the signature F, the fabric was perfect for day into evening bags. Anne Klein's shaped clutch also made the most of black, with a single, scalloped top and gilt trim. More gregarious evening bags were made in acid colors, such as the small, 1988 lime green, satin drawstring pouch, trimmed with suede, by Miss Maud of NYC.

Bags as Fashion Statements

By 1986, handbags were mimicking the vogue for gilt chains. Large cluttered jewelry, chunky chain belts, jangling bracelets, and big earrings were worn with endless gilt chained variations on the handbag. Karl Lagerfeld for Chanel, the originator of the most famous gilt chained, quilted leather bag, made credit card-sized versions in scarlet leather, tasseled white leather, fuchsia jersey, and black leather, as well as white canvas drawstring shoulder bags—all with entwined gilt and leather chain straps.

As bags became increasingly decorative, Byblos' shoulder bag with gilt chain bag in rococo, printed chintz with leather trimming appeared. Koos van den Akker, the American designer born in the

The return of the reptile

Reptile skins, real and fake, enjoyed a huge revival in the 1980s, but with a new pzazz. The conventional, polished leather handbag in browns and russets, such as La Bagagerie's saddlebag in chestnut brown lizard or small, dark grey, fake crocodile shoulder bags of 1980 were joined by reptile skin bags of alligator, crocodile, snake, lizard, or eelskin. Many were dyed vibrant shades of neon blues, pinks, yellows, and purples.

Patchworks of reptile skin, sometimes dyed in shades such as lilac, purple, and red, appeared early in the decade, and Enny anticipated the trend with shiny, small, red, faux crocodile shoulder bags. By 1986, many bright colored bags were made from embossed leather imitating reptile skins, from blue alligator basket totes by the American company Kleinberg Sherrill to embossed, red and orange cowhide binocular cases and half moon bags from fellow Americans Green Mountain.

Although fake reptile bags were seen everywhere, the real thing was still on sale too. Emerald, crocodile drawstring pouches made by the British company Lederer, who had been around since the 1950s, sold alongside bright white crocodile shoulder bags with chains by Chanel in 1986. Carlos Falchi's glazed, brown alligator clutch could be bought at Henri Bendel, in New York, as could slim, ostrich wallets and black crocodile passport cases made exclusively for Barney's of New York.

Long-handled tote, rucksack with side zip and organizer in naturally tanned "vintage 38 leather", handcrafted in the USA by Ghurka, 1980s.

This lady-like, black leather handbag with shaped flap and short, finger-held straps, designed by Moschino, is accessorized with pearls spilling from its interior, scarf, carnations, and bizarrely, green foliage, to create the context for a definitive fashion statement.

Netherlands who was famous for his gaily patterned, collaged clothes, added a cheerful line of handbags in 1986.

Towards the late 1980s, small, structured bags emerged, such as the geometric black and white patterned bags by the American Jill Stuart. Her compatriot Anne Klein produced bags and belts that were sharper and more dazzling, such as her clutch bag with large polka dots and flap front, as did Donna Karan with her shaped and structured shoulder bags and clutches.

But it was a large, flat, yellow bag by Mondi, with short shoulder straps that crossed over the bag in a huge black cross, which seemed to signal the direction that modern bags were taking. Although the French designer Paloma Picasso said of accessories in the 1980s that they "should reflect classicism as well as a sense of timelessness," bag design was to gradually move away from the classic tone of the 1980s. Working hard for women as they did, bags had rarely taken off on flights of fancy. They had to wait for the 1990s for that.

Bright, red leather shoulder bag and matching shoe by Charles Jourdan. The angular shape of the pointed sides of bag and large flap are also reflected by the narrow-shaped high heel with v-shaped cut out. Red is for danger!

123

Ghurka business bag (*left*) in chestnut leather, and holdall by Dooney & Bourke (*right*)..

A collection of Charles Jourdan travel bags (*below*).

Suitcases and Traveling Bags

The history and design of travel baggage is strongly tied in with social change, for it is shaped by the dramatic developments in transportation which this century has seen.

A selection of Ghurka travel bags (above).Each one is stamped with its own serial number and the initials of the Ghurka designer, Marley Hodgson.

Different methods of transportation and the ways in which people travel, affect both the style and the size of baggage.

In the early decades of the century, travel had an epic quality to it. People who could afford to do so moved around with enormous amounts of baggage, holding endless changes of clothing and associated accessories. Numerous servants were required to pack and unpack the vast amounts of baggage, which could well have been made by Louis Vuitton, the most famous maker of distinctive baggage, both then and today. Vuitton's gray, Trianon canvas-covered trunks were highly complex, with interiors that included clothes rails and drawers to stop the clothes creasing.

In the 1920s and 1930s, Italian aristocrats and European royalty also patronized the Italian company Fratelli Prada, who were established in 1913 by Mario Prada and made luxury trunks and suitcases. The suitcases, made from walrus skin, were extremely heavy, their fitted compartments filled with tortoiseshell, ivory, and gold toilet accessories.

As early as the 1930s, when flying was in its infancy, the Italian designer Elsa Schiaparelli responded to the challenge to produce lightweight travel accessories. She created "an entire trousseau in a specially designed Constellation bag weighing less than10lbs (22 kg), including a reversible coat for day and night, six dresses and three hats," as she wrote in her autobiography, *Shocking Life*.

Travel became much more available to all following the postwar boom of the 1950s, and holidays became the norm. Casual weekends away gave rise to casual styles of baggage that could be squashed into the back of the car. Lord & Taylor of the U.S. sold a large weekend holdall of off-white cowhide bound in black, which was featured in *Vogue* in 1951. By 1954, a Brooke Cadwallader carryall in black

and white print, with room enough inside for an overnight wardrobe, was available from Ronay at Saks Fifth Avenue.

Handbags too, were adapted for traveling. Cosmetic travel cases had been made ever since make-up had become big business. But it was the new, lightweight materials available for baggage makers to work with that really revolutionized the luggage scene. New tanning techniques were absorbed into pouched and leather-lined travel handbags of soft lightweight calfskin, made by Abe Silver of New York in 1958, and

similar pieces of baggage. Gaston Vuitton (grandson of Louis) developed a petrochemical compound to coat cotton canvas in 1959, resulting in a durable, strong but lightweight material to withstand the trauma of traveling.

Fabric treated in this way could also be stamped with the Vuitton monogram, and the resulting Vuitton "Steamer" and "Keepall" established a new era for travel bags with designer logos. Even their washable vinyl exteriors were imitated as other designers followed with their own initialed fabric bags, including the House of Dior. Their "Globetrotters" became the favorite lightweight luggage of foreign correspondents, and are almost indestructible.

By the 1960s, the handbag and cosmetic case were often united, and leather bags which could be folded away to nothing also became fashionable. A Gucci packable pigskin handbag in dark brown, leather-lined and with many compartments, featured in a 1961 version of U.S.

Circular vanity bag (*above*) in black leather with zip fastener, 1996.

Vogue. There was not another major shift in baggage design until the 1970s, with the mass production of tough, soft vinyl products. Among these were the "Sherbrooke Handi-Tote", from Samsonite, which had zippered pockets, a ticket pocket, lock closing, and accompanying "Petit Tote". Such plasticized fabrics were ideal for the lightweight, unstructured, baggage which was made in the 1990s by Delsey and Antler, as well as Samsonite. More expensive, and even tougher, are bags by American makes such as Andiamo, Hartmann, and Tumi.

Throughout the century, the great luggage houses continued to make rigid suitcases and trunks, including Tanner Krolle, who established their family business in London in 1856. Their expanding suitcases, each of which is made from start to finish by one craftsman alone, in vegetable tanned leather, and finished with solid brass fittings, still sell for enormous sums. In contrast, the Franchetti Bond range, brightly colored, waxed leather bags designed by Baronessa Mariangela Franchetti, which bear the family crest, are rather more affordable, even though they incorporate top level Italian craftsmanship.

"*Boite pharmacie*" (traveler's medicine chest), by Louis Vuitton (*left*) from the early decades of the century.

"Berkley" designs by Bill
Amberg (*right*).

"Landscape" (*below*), in
smooth bridle leather, with
bamboo-print leather
handles

Bill Amberg

From childhood play with scraps of leather, Amberg
learned his trade from leatherworkers around the world,
before setting up what was to become an international
business in London.

Amberg's black leather
storage boxes (*above*).

Bill Amberg was born in
Northamptonshire, the home
of the English leather trade,
and designed his first wallets
and bags as a child after being given
some scraps of leather. His interest in
the material remained, and he went
on to travel the world, apprenticing
himself to leatherworkers wherever he
went. After some years in Australia,
he returned to Britain in 1983 and set
up his leather design business and
shop in London.

From the beginning, he worked with
some of the top names in the industry.
He enrolled as a consultant for the
designers Donna Karan, Romeo Gigli,
Margaret Howell, and Coach Leather,
and designed and developed exclusive
ranges for Browns Own Label. He sold
his wares in major British stores, from
Harrods, Browns, Harvey Nichols,
Selfridges, and Liberty, to the Conran
Shop. He specialized in creating
corporate designs for Apple
Computers, Sony, Virgin Music, and
other multinational companies. Today,

Amberg's exports to the U.S. and
Japan account for over 60 percent of
his business.

Amberg's quirky, minimalist style
emerged early on, blending traditional
leather craftsmanship with the
requirements of modern living, work,
travel, and leisure. His functional,
purposeful bags were soon found in
many major stores, designed as often
as not for the working man or woman.
The interior of his 1989 "Tillman"
case, in matte wax leather, formed a
detailed mobile office, while the
"buckled envelope" was part of a
corporate collection in buffalo calf
leather. Smooth, minimal briefcases
were set off by details, such as cast
aluminum handles which closed with
the aid of a magnet.

In the 1980s, Amberg produced a
range of more casual designs,
including the "jug" duffel. Initially
designed in leather for Paul Smith, the
bag was also made in lightweight
ripstop sailcloth or bright cottons, and
carried either as a suitcase or over the

shoulder. Amberg has often married leather with other materials, as seen on the "body belt" for the urban nomad. The bag was attached to a thick buckled belt with contrasting stitching, decorated by panels of Liberty print fabrics and fake animal furs.

Some of Amberg's designs were at the cutting edge of chain store fashion, including the fringed suede bags he designed for Whistles in the 1990s, and zippered, unstructured bags for Joseph and Jigsaw. More practical were his nylon duffel bags for the Conran Shop and Space U.K., and by 1996, the BAN range (Bill Amberg Nylons) included a washbag and jug duffel bag, in red, navy, and green tartan. Amberg's large, soft, shoulder bags with v-shaped flaps also appeared, the interiors lined with his new signature lining of jacquard-weave fabrics designed in association with Paul Vogel.

Bill Amberg's success is in part thanks to his versatility. He has made desk sets in cornerstitched English bridle leather—which included a cufflinks box, a floppy disc box, and covers and bags for computers—and romantic wallets in handpainted python skin of peacock, gold, silver, and burgundy. His evening bags include the "Berkeley", in printed suede with silver-plated handles, and others in gold drawstring. Padded and quilted shoppers, openwork carriers, dainty, check handbags, micro-wallets, and the "Venetian" case with handcast glass handles in purple, lime, orange, and black, have all brought him acclaim.

Amberg's love of his chosen material is evident in all his work. In a white vellum jewelry cabinet of 1995, the precision that leather is capable of is seen in the way that the corners are defined, as if smoothed with the fingertips. His designs include leather in almost any situation, resulting in leather chairs, leather-topped tables, molded leather bowls, warm and hardwearing leather floors.

Yet the handbag remains the perfect vehicle for his talents. Among his best

known are those in English bridle leather with bamboo-print leather handles, named the "Portrait", the "Landscape", and the "Gladstone". Formed and smoothed by hand, and then worn in by its owner, the bag takes on the perfume and the personality of each woman who owns one. In Amberg's mind, this is the sophisticated woman with a good eye. The curiously personal and intimate nature of the handbag, the fact that it has a distinct interior and exterior, that women take as much delight in its secret side as in its public one, appeals to Bill Amberg, who argues that we probably use bags more regularly than any other item of clothing. But for him, the "passion is for leather, not fashion."

A selection of clutch bags and purse handmade in Bill Amberg's London workshops, 1996. One is in orange leather and the other three in handpainted python made in Italy.

Long "Portrait" bag in English bridle leather, is one of Amberg's most well-known designs.

Substantial weekend/business bag (*left*) bound , brass fittings, and name tag, and women's travel bag (below), with zip top, double handles, and outside pocket for tickets.

Louis Vuitton

The son of a country carpenter became an expert packer of voluminous nineteenth-century dresses, and then combined his skills to become the foremost designer of luxury baggage.

In 1851, Louis Vuitton, the son of a carpenter, traveled on foot from the Jura mountains on the borders of northern France and Germany, to Paris. He became an apprentice trunkpacker, packing the ornate, hooped dresses of the time for wealthy and aristocratic women. Three years later, he branched out on his own, combining the woodworking skills acquired from his carpenter father and his first-hand experience of the packing problems of the rich. He began to design and make luxury trunks. In the late 1800s, traditional trunks for long journeys by steamer were round topped. Vuitton developed a new, sophisticated style of flat topped trunk, with the great advantage of being able to be stacked. The first Vuitton trunks were covered

Sculptural handbag with adjustable shoulder strap, rounded flap echoing the base, and enhanced by parallel curved line pattern, c.1980s.

in Trianon gray canvas, which gave them a distinctive air of elegance. They certainly appealed to Empress Eugènie and her Court, and helped the young Vuitton gain his first awards for design at the 1867 Universal Exhibition.

Branching Out

From 1875, Vuitton made wardrobe trunks, lined with Moroccan leather. They were fitted with hangers and leather-handled, removable drawers in which clothes could be laid, was provided by Louis's son, Georges, when he invented the five tumbler lock. Theftproof and with a personalized number for each owner, the lock is still in use today. George also introduced the monogram-patterned canvas in 1896, with intertwined LV initials and simple flower shapes, which is still used in Vuitton collections today. The pattern helped to prevent counterfeiting which was rife at the time, and it also made Vuitton's luggage immediately identifiable.

In 1959, Louis's grandson Gaston Vuitton developed a new chemical process to coat the monogrammed

canvas with a durable, waterproof layer. It was ideal for using in both flexible and rigid luggage, and was adopted by many top leather and fashion houses.

Early Vuitton designs for hand luggage, such as the "Steamer" of 1901 and the "Keepall" of 1924 were the forerunners of modern luggage, while the "Speedy" bag, a soft, light handbag in monogrammed canvas, is still made today. The first Noé bag, a drawstring duffel style with cord threaded through rivets, and a shoulder strap, was made in 1932, as a special commission by a champagne house to hold five bottles of champagne. It is believed to have inspired the open leather bucket bag, so popular in the 1950s.

Faithful to Origins

Recent years have seen Louis Vuitton once again at the top of the fashion market in both quality and styling. The 1980s preoccupation with designer labels and logos meant that owning a genuine Vuitton bag is a real status symbol. The company continues to cater for the luxury market as it has done since its

inception. Bags in the 80s included the "Bebe St Cloud" natural tan leather shoulder bag, with buckle and topstitching. For the successful career woman there were EPI rigid box briefcases in grained leather lined in calf, handmade and finished, with a matching portfolio that fitted inside. These cost $2,200 in 1986.

Handbags of the early 90s included Morocco leather, drawstring duffel bags, and business card cases. Zip topped shoppers followed, which were wider at the top than at the base. In 1994, the fashion for brilliant colours, after seasons of black, resulted in the "Sac Triangle" in maize yellow, and the "Cannes" bag in Technicolor red.

The revival of the saddlebag and fieldbag in 1996, led to casual, hip-length styles, U-haped and with a single, thin strap. In the same year Vuitton revived the Damier check canvas, which was originally designed in 1888 by Louis Vuitton, and featured it in a large, boxy rucksack with buckled flap and leather trimmings. The signing of Marc Jacobs in 1997 to design for the label has resulted in bold, minimalist designs

A selection of canvas-printed designs with LV pattern (*clockwise from top left*): large tote, suitcase with reinforced rounded corners, weekend shoulder bag, drawstring holdall sack, 1980s weekend bag with shoulder strap, and unstructured weekender with buckle fastener.

such as the square "Males herbes" and the "Epi" leather in yellow or red with flapfront and short handle.

Louis Vuitton have the authority and confidence of well over 100 years of luggage and bagmaking. While they will always remain solidly famous as the first name in luxury luggage, and still continue to make trunks and wardrobes for those not intending to fly to their destinations, their fashionable accessories also have the quality of an investment. Vuitton bags transcend fashion—they are so handsome, and so well designed that they last through many a season.

Large, spacious, shoulder bag, navy and white canvas with red trimming on outer edges, Gucci.

Gucci

Gucci may not be particularly known for innovative design, but a bag with the double "G" logo is coveted as a symbol of high-profile street credibility and, until the 90s, at least, for enduring classic styles.

Simple,small, drawstring tote/shoulder bag in white, includes additional outside pocket and Gucci logo.

With branches all over Europe and the US, from Honolulu to Las Vegas, Gucci's Italian handbags and accessories have captured the hearts of women worldwide. The company was founded in the 1920s, originally as a saddlemakers, but made its mark in the world of handbags with a distinctive, bamboo-handled bag in 1957.

Gucci's global profile grew with the 1980s introduction of the double "G" logo. It appeared on side-zippered shoulder bags, in leather, and canvas printed with Gucci's entwined double initials, on initialed key rings, and on evening and cocktail bags. Typical of the evening bags was the exotic, green lizard cocktail bag of 1984, which had a curved frame and thick silk knotted cord handle with tassels.

American sales of Gucci wares expanded in the 1980s with a series of shrewd advertising campaigns emphasizing the element of free choice, which is so important to the independent American market. "We realize that Gucci cannot dictate a personal style," the patter ran, but "When you visit our stores or look through our catalog, however, you will be able to choose the style that suits your personal taste." Photo-shoots for Gucci shoes, belts, wallets, and bag collections, located on the North Eastern coast of the U.S.A. were directed at the casual, relaxed American market, featuring cool, fresh, bright white shoes, crocodile bags, and casual clothing.

While recognizing that the days of one bag were over, and that women were choosing a variety of interesting bags and changing them daily, Gucci continued to sell its own classics well into the 1990s. Purses with gilt hand clasps, casual, topstitched country shoulder bags in tan and cream leather, and suede and leather rucksacks were all in production, as well as tiny bags with bamboo handles that satisfied the rage for miniaturization of the early 1990s.

Sturdy, practical, brown leather Gucci bag with a logo-covered canvas front and striped green and red panel.

was pretty substantial too. Simple, oversize camel pony bags wide enough at the base to stand on their own were marketed alongside short strap shoulder bags which rested on the hip.

Towards the end of the 1990s, the changes in Gucci styles were largely due to the designer Tom Ford. His 1997 handbags as flat as pancakes were mirrored by flat, square handbags made from metal mesh with long, thin straps. Sleek versions of earlier, oversize sacks appeared, superseding totes and duffels with the new, large, flat envelopes worn asymmetrically across the body. As always, the elegant, distinctive bags and their accessories struck a chord with women around the globe.

Witty, bright, diminutive and sweet, these miniature bags existed side by side with their larger siblings, their satisfyingly high quality even more apparent in their scale. Many cosmetic companies even reduced the size of their products' packaging to fit into the new bags.

Among Gucci's many winning designs of the early 1990s was the slouch bag, which was both substantial and glamorous, especially the ones made of gold leather in 1993. Day bags in real crocodile skin, with brisk snap fastenings and a bamboo handle, were sold in 1994, alongside the smoothest of brown leather shoulder bags with heavy brass strap fittings and plain front fastening. Gucci's cerise, ocher, and mustard rucksacks of the same year had a bamboo carrying handle, and were flap-fronted. The outside pockets had a bamboo swivel fastening.

A new minimalism appeared in the bags of the mid 1990s, the finest leathers to their best advantage, with no distracting gilt and top stitching. One handbag of 1996, shiny and flat, with a perfect oval cut out for the handle, was so large that it covered the naked model holding it; its cost, over one thousand American dollars,

Unique, simple, red leather bag with logo-covered front panel below a navy stripe with two Gucci "G"s on either side.

The Accessorized Millennium

By the early 1990s, designers had recognized the power of the accessory. Women were spending more on such accessories as bags, hats, and shoes, and they became an integral part of catwalk collections. Bags and hats enlivened the minimalist outfits of the 1990s, packing a punch of color and wit, and designer accessories soon dominated many longer established bag manufacturers. While some bags radicalized otherwise classic outfits, others were also used for visual continuity, many reworking the earlier Kelly bag, originally by Hermès, and the famous 2.55 inches quilted chain bag by Chanel. By 1994, the number of things that women were carrying seemed to have increased, not decreased. Tongue-in-cheek ideas as to how to cope with modern life sprung up, with Karl Lagerfeld's gilt and leather, chain, bottled water carrier for Chanel, and his bejeweled portable phone. Muji's understated strong canvas "three-way" bag was designed to carry the latest in laptop computer technology, and Asprey's made bespoke attaché cases.

Naomi Campbell (*above*), wearing a typical mid 90s leopard skin dress, shows that accessories are a vital part of the total look, while the bag (*right*) is typical of the designs that give a lift to minimalist 90s fashion.

DKNY's practical, oblong
leather shopping bag
(*above*)—large and capacious
for daytime use.

A MIXED MODERN BAG

Some designer created their own accessories, rather than just licencing their name, while others commissioned talented handbag designers to come up with complementary bags. Donna Karan, originally a womenswear designer, was one who expanded into accessories, and her DKNY range included bags which were sold from DKNY outlets in America and London, as well as from stores such as Marshall Field's in New York.

In Britain, the extraordinary designer Vivienne Westwood had long been using accessories to accentuate her designs. In 1992, she accessorized her printed cotton drill jacket and satin corset and shorts with a large, drawstring, Boucher print bag, while a 1993 micro-kilt and fake fur cape outfit was shown in *Vogue* with a clutch doggie bag designed especially for Westwood by Braccialini.

In Paris, Isabel Canovas, a former accessory designer for Vuitton and Dior, opened a boutique selling her bi-annual collections of accessories; one year, perhaps with a glance to Schiaparelli, these included an exquisite circus tent bag complete with striped awning and miniature circus figure. Equally interesting were the small bags in John Galliano's master collection for Dior in 1997, his red Indian look reinforced by a brightly beaded, geometrically patterned, drawstring bag. Its shape was reminiscent of the early century, and it came complete with cord and tassel.

Many smaller companies also built on their successes in the accessory loving 1990s. The French company, La Bagagerie, expanded into America, while in Britain, Russell & Bromley provided a middle ground between named and mass-produced bags with their quality design and manufacture. The recently formed Dollargrand filled another gap in the market with their chic, affordable bags, and Jane Shilton, a British company, active for many decades, found a worldwide market for their Clubhouse collection of navy and red leather handbags trimmed with yellow braid. Saddlery companies such as Coach Leather and Mulberry also expanded, but still left room for individualistic designers such as American, Kate Spade, and Britain's Bill Amberg.

Making the Most of the Choice

Women were buying more than just one classic bag, spending not only for investment or as a rushed afterthought, but to provide their wardrobe with a positive, bright dash of color and shape. As bags were not too costly to be changed around daily, they took on a new duality, being both practical and pleasurable.

Early in the 1990s, bulging totes and small, ladylike bags were the clear alternatives for women, who could always carry both, as in

A Longchamp bucket bag
(*left*)—a stylistic
throwback to the 1950s.

Unusually shaped beauty box and discus bags (*above*) of synthetic, pewter grey satin—for evening wear, but often used during the day, Jane Shilton, Autumn 1995.

Top-of-the-range shopping bag (*above*) from Jane Shilton's Spring Collection in overtly fake python printed hide with a simple, elegant shape.

Fur to the fore

Designers have always loved animal prints and fur, returning to them again and again in their collections. Animal prints furnished homes, accessories, clothes, shoes, and bags, and in the eco-conscious 1990s, fake sold better than a real skin unless it was either reworked or a natural by-product.

The small scale of accessories lent itself to such overwhelming prints, and added luxury to otherwise minimal outfits. Zipper-topped, leather backpacks by Esprit in 1990 had imitation panther fur pocket bags, and mock croc Kelly bags went on sale in 1991 from Mila Schön. Fake fur and animal prints were hot for winter bags, belts, sunglasses, mini skirts, and even hair bands. Faux reptile skin was very popular, although some top handbag houses continued to use real reptile skins on bags for the wealthy and guilt-free.

In 1997, tortoiseshell enjoyed a renaissance, very occasionally as the real thing but more often in mottled plastic. Gucci and Prada both featured bag straps in mock tortoiseshell, and Osborne & Little produced a tortoiseshell wallpaper print.

the 1980s. Bags for daytime use were often large and practical, such as DKNY's oblong, leather shopping bags, and bucket bags influenced by a revival of 1950s styles. There were patent leather bags by French designer Philip Model, the characteristic woven leather bags of Bottega Veneta, and Special Edition smooth, leather handbags by Coach, which were half the price of those from the most costly designers. At the top end of the market were Fratelli Rossetti of New York, London, and Paris—"A certain world walks in Rossetti" ran their advertising slogan—while younger brands such as NafNaf, Snoopy, and Morgan provided bags in bright colors and cheap prices for those with less to spend.

Small, Neat and Swinging Bags

The movement towards neat, swinging, ladylike bags started in the early 1990s. These were not necessarily structured, and encompassed shoulder bags made by Laurel in green with a navy blue border, and Perry Ellis's shoulderstrap bag of soft, smooth leather with a drawstring, flap top, and zippered pockets. Small, neat shoulder bags were made by Sonia Rykiel, and handheld bags included Mercedes Robirosa's Clover bag and Chloe's 1992 small, nubuck bag with zipper, to be worn with Shetland colored knits and tartan suits.

Valentino's green leather bags, red lizard bags by Ferragamo, green and yellow leather handbags by Celine, and small, red leather bags by The Coach Store all had neat, stiff handles and compact bodies, as did Yves St Laurent's dressy, gilt bracelet

Day bags (*above*) from The Bridge or Il Ponte—an Italian-based, fine leather goods company—made from supple, woven leather.

Model (*above right*) sporting a Moschino, gold, leather shoulder bag with metal links, Spring 1997.

handled bag of 1991. Different but also stylish was Chanel's overarm chain bag, worn over the shoulder with the bag tucked high under the arm, while the glamorous end of the market was filled by bags such as Gucci's gold leather slouch of 1993, Red or Dead's gold leather shoppers, or bright, metallic, silver and gold leather handbags from companies such as Dollargrand.

A Need for Nostalgia

In the 1990s, the saddlery tradition which started in Europe and America in the 19th century was revitalized by young American companies such as Dooney & Bourke, Coach, and the British company Mulberry. The success of such enterprises indicated that a yearning for country pursuits still remained in the heart of every town dweller.

Fishing rods, baskets, and fallen leaves dominated the advertisements of Dooney & Bourke, placing their bags in a setting of rural innocence. Such a promotion may have been effective in selling their product, but belied its sophistication. Despite its

Grunge: the antithesis of glamor

The alternative mores of the subcultural grunge movement hit the catwalks in the early 1990s, and by 1993, cheap, popular versions of young, grunge styles were being sold in shopping malls and department stores across America and Britain. But despite being alternative, grunge was still accessorized. Jewelry typically consisted of thong necklaces or bracelets, and old working boots or scruffy trainers were worn on the feet. Anything crocheted was in, from hats, belts, and beanies to gloves, and crochet was found on bags such as

French design company Jamin Puech's crocheted backpacks.

Fringed, suede bags by Joseph in 1997 continued to show the influence of grunge, which was only truly successful in styles for the very young, although many designers tried to incorporate the look in their clothes. This differed from earlier young street styles, from the Swinging Sixties to punk in the 1970s, which had greatly influenced top designers.

But older, couture customers were more cautious about grunge, their concerns voiced by designer Rifat Ozbek: "You get out of bed and put on whatever's on the floor next to you. Isn't that what grunge is?" Such a reaction to grunge styles and dressing down lent weight to the move towards more ladylike handbags that was soon underway.

Red, leather day bags and belt (*above*) from Longchamp —their distinctive, embossed logo of a horse and rider can be seen on each bag flap.

Classic, Italian bag and briefcase (*right*) from The Bridge in supple leather, tanned using natural ingredients for longevity and quality, 1990s.

saddlestitching and sturdy appearance, very few female anglers would carry such a finely made bag.

The truth was that such handbags contained pretty much what any other woman's handbag held—keys, money, make-up, spectacles, diary—rather than worms, hooks, and sandwiches for lunch. Like many fashion accessories, country handbags were an idealistic anachronism, harking after rural honesty, a lack of sophistication and healthy day pursuits rather than providing them.

The bag's durability did fit into the idea of a bag as a classic investment, however, with all the associations of power, sex, and money that this brought with it. As U.S. *Vogue* commented in 1994, "Once considered ultraconservative, saddle leather has become a staple for the chic set. Fashioned into everything from strappy stilettos to structured handbags, this cognac-colored hide announces a new breed of sexy accessories that retain a classic image while bucking tradition." The article featured bags by Calvin Klein, Carolina Herrera Accessories, Paloma Picasso Couture and Daniel Swarovski.

Companies such as Dooney & Bourke, Coach and Mulberry were briefly caught between the really old-established, saddlery companies such as Tanner Krolle, and the giants of the couture world. Their shorter roots meant that some newer country handbag firms were tempted to move into high fashion. But those that survived did so because they offered stylish value for money, even if they did become increasingly removed from the predominating fashions, from grunge and minimalism to the romantic.

Some, like Mulberry, branched out into clothing, creating a complete look for their bags. Others, like Coach, remained hugely successful because their design team was always one step ahead (and widely copied), without abandoning their signature look. Thanks to the flexibility of fashion, which accomodates numerous looks at the same time, they continued to prosper.

Matching sets return again

The continuing dilemma of little bags versus large ones led to handbags being teamed up with purse-size versions yet again. Such "mother and baby" sets were made by upmarket companies such as Chanel—their 1994 bags and purses in quilted leather or tweed were designed to match the Chanel suit. Ferragamo's bag had crisp snap fastenings on their matching sets of plain leather bags and purses on metal frames. In 1993, Dior produced their own suede Gladstones with a mini bag attached.

This bag (*above*), in chocolate and white leather, is typical of the wit of the Moschino Collection and demonstrates a melted chocolate design—a collector's item. Summer 1996.

A New Femininity

Handbag designers took full advantage of the new mood of romanticism that swept fashionable salons in the very early 1990s. Although some women feared that sweet and dainty bags would undermine the progress they had made in being taken seriously in their professions, others argued that they were confident enough to possess bags that were both practical and frivolous. By 1994, small handbags were well and truly back, happpily co-existing alongside backpacks and totes.

In Britain, the climate was right to receive newly emerging designers such as Anya Hindmarch. Her 1992 small, ladylike bags in pastel satins were decorated with jewels, and featured novelties such as gilt poodles. Cosmetic companies began making tiny versions of make-up. For the autumn/winter collection of 1994, fellow Briton Bella Freud featured the super thin supermodel Kate Moss in twinset and bucket bag trimmed with marabou. Her sexy, ladylike fashions reminded women of 1950s stars such as Audrey Hepburn and Grace Kelly, and handbags had became the focus of attention once again.

Fashion journalists, handbag buyers, and socialites agreed that a more tailored look was back, and that women were again choosing accessories to finish off outfits. The handbag, a symbol of female sexuality, was said to be "like the high heel. It is the last bastion of femininity, something men just can't get away with." But it was so long since handbags had been sexy that many women did not know how to carry one. Young women had to learn how to manipulate their handbags, place them down carefully, open them with style, and snap them shut.

Lime green, leather day bag (*below*) by Esprit reflecting the fashion for bright, acidic colors teamed with the contemporary feel for clean, uncluttered lines, 1990s.

Patrick Cox Spring/Summer 1997 advertisement (*above*) featuring the romantic look with lilac, capretto leather handbag and matching high-heeled, ankle-strap shoes.

White, leather evening bag (*above*) with large, gilt bracelet handle by Magli—reminiscent of the boxy, feminine styles of the 1950s.

Woven handbag (*above*) by Ferragamo giving a simple, elegant, textured design, Spring/Summer 1997.

Modern and smoothly contoured, this white day bag (*below*) by Ferragamo has a single, short handle which is tubular—complementing the bag's uncluttered lines.

Sweeping the Catwalk

Delightful, diminutive, and newly feminine, 1950s influenced bags swept the catwalk shows. There were quilted box bags by MaxMara and glittery ones by Chloe. Chanel made quilted, calf fur skin boxes with rigid chain handle and Miu Miu, tweed boxes with leather handles. One of the dominant proponents of the new ladylike look was British designer Lulu Guinness, whose fans included tall Texan model Jerry Hall, who was seen with Guinness' 'daisy' bucket bag in 1994.

Those who wanted a totally coordinated look could buy a Michel Klein belt, bag, and gloves in matching print, while ladylike Hermès bags with small handles and the large, gilt signature 'H' were featured with suede gloves studded with gold. Of course there were some customers who had continued to buy matching bags and

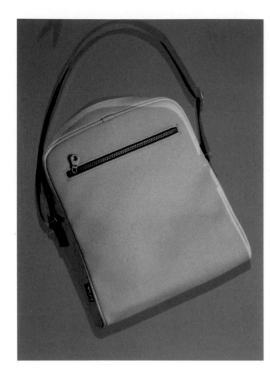

Paul Smith handbag (*above*)
in pale blue leather with side
zip and slim strap, 1997.

Patrick Cox handbags (*above*) with matching capretto leather clutch bag and
belt. Made of embossed leather to give colored "mosaic" effect,
Spring/Summer Collection, 1997.

gloves while fashion had gone full circle. Dents, makers of traditional
English leather accessories since 1777, had steadfastly supplied
leather handbags and gloves in black and navy to those for whom the
original, conventional market had never changed.

NOSTALGIA VERSUS MODERNITY

Black and white leather handbags (*above*)
from Goldpfeil—meaning "golden arrow"—
the company's logo of an arrow can be seen
in these designs.

The lady-like look overlapped with, but intrinsically differed from, the romantic look, a stalwart in British fashion which had been exported to America so successfully by Laura Ashley. The romantic look in the 1990s had a hard edge to it, however, that was summed up by the 1997 advertisements of British shoe and bag maker Patrick Cox. They featured a model with tousled, curly hair sprawled on a bed in her 1930s looking, chiffon, flowered dress, still wearing her high-heeled shoes and clutching her handbag.

Nostalgic, printed fabrics and longer skirt lengths inspired by collections of designers such as English Eccentrics, accompanied by satin bags with large, hand-painted tulips by Carolina Herrera, and silk bags with tiny rose passementerie trimmings by Erick. Lulu Guinness' rose-covered bucket bags were the epitomy of the refined, romantic look, the neat precision of the satin bucket complementing perfectly the satin and velvet, rose-covered lids.

Antique purses came back into vogue, their styles imitated in Edwardian-looking, chain mail bags by British designer Anya Hindmarch, rose print bags from Dolce & Gabbana, and Anne Sui tapestry bags.

Bags (*left*) from the Ladies Handbag Collection at Daks—includes the mini and medium Monaco bag, made of embossed leather, to resemble ostrich skin.

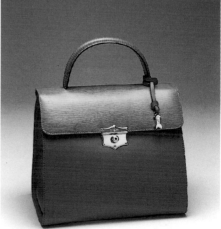

A scattering of simple and stylish purses (*above*) by Longchamp in blue, red and brown colors, made of nylon with leather trims and press stud fastenings.

In contrast, a new taste for minimalism and modernity in fashion took shape in the "nude" bag styles of designers such as Bill Amberg, Dollargrand and Jil Sander. They specialized in using leather and other materials without excessive hardwear, both in bright and subtle shades.

High gloss bags in acidic colors appeared in 1995, their shapes modern and sharp. Vinyl was in—for shoes, narrow belts, bags, and coats—and there were scarlet, patent leather shopping bags by Yves St Laurent Rive Gauche and laminated Vogue cover clutch bags by British designers at Paul Smith Women. All provided clean, feminine accents without being "pretty."

A brief vogue for 1960s style, complete with short, flared trousers and formal suits updated for the 1990s, led to a spate of accessories, including long-handled, overarm bags. The sharp shapes and colors of the bags were set off by gloves in purple, lilac, and mint green nylon, which also added an increased formality to the overall look.

The Hepburnesque suits required hats, strappy shoes, and neat bags in vibrant colors, provided by Lulu Guinness' orange satin bag or suede, mini shoppers from Dollargrand. Simple shapes emerged, such as Sonia Rykiel's cut-out handle bag in patent leather, and when a bag was not neon bright, it was generally transparent in clear plastic and PVC. See-through bags from Prada came with opaque purses, while Salvatore Ferragamo and Chanel made rigid, transparent bags with gilt clasps and a top handle, like updated versions of 1950s, American, molded plastic bags.

Tan leather handbag (*above*) with short handle—capacious and practical, the rounded flap fastens with a briefcase style lock. Hanging from the handle is a brass arrow, the logo of Goldpfeil, 1990s.

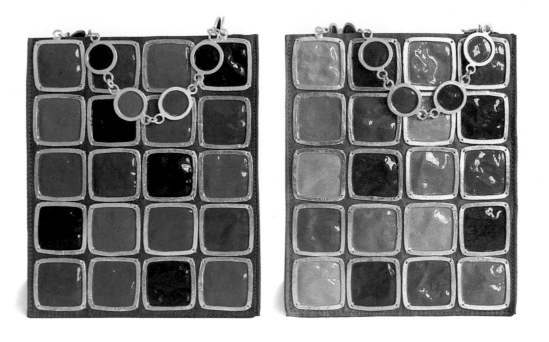

Colorful, silk evening bags (*right*) with enamelled, metal panels, sewn by hand onto a silk base—inspired by the work of painter, Alastair MacKillop, and designed by Emily Jo Gibbs, 1997.

Lemon, yellow day bag (*below*) by Paul Smith, made of nappa leather with rigid handle. Brown shoulder bag (*below right*) with a large gilt M—for Magli—a reworking of the classic croc day bag in a more informal style, 1996.

Staying Power of the Shoulder Bag

The short strap bag returned in 1996, tucked closely against the body, and small, handheld bags suddenly felt like a liability. Gucci and Paul Smith Women, among others, softened its outline into a square or U shape, while Dolce & Gabbana made a glossy, patent version with thin straps.

Before long, the short strap shoulder bag got larger, with oversized bags from Bagatelle, black, tricotine bags from Prada, green felt and leather by Hermès and black calf bags by Bill Blass Couture. These were superseded by an enormous bag with an oval cut out for a handle by Gucci, in shiny smooth calf. There was yet another surge of interest in chain bags—a continuing tribute to the Chanel classic of

1955—and 1996 versions included Bottega Veneta's fine, pin-striped bag with linked chain and Renaud Pellegrino's metallic, leather clutch with an ornate, looped, chain handle. Even Chanel looked again at the design, with quilted cloth bags having a twisted leather and gilt chain.

Fortuna Valentino launched a snakeskin bag with a dense, short chain, saying: "Women want something classic, but they also want something precious. This is a great time for accessories. Clothes are so simple, and using a bag with a chain is two accessories in one—an alternative to wearing a gold chain around your neck or wrist."

The Right Bag for Summer

Straw has long been a favorite choice for designers working on summer bags, and the early 1990s were no exception. Woven, synthetic straw baskets with plexi handles could be made to order from Karl Lagerfeld, and British designer Sonia Rykiel produced a range of little straw bags and black taffetta, drawstring bags.

For the beach, there were Dolce & Gabbana straw bikinis and beach bags, wicker bags to go with Lacroix's suits with raffia fringing and string, crochet vests, and raffia-covered bags by Eric Beamon—adorned with objects found on the beach. Jean-Paul Gaultier's straw bucket bag of 1992 featured a natural leather handle, while Yves St Laurent Rive Gauche made little purse bags in cotton macramé with cord drawstring.

Always lighthearted, straw bags were becoming more humorous by 1994. Young, American designer, Kate Spade, said of her raffia-fringed burlap Hula bag, which she designed for Todd Oldham, that "summer bags should be small and humorous...it's like something Mary Ann from Gilligan's Island would have worn." Jamin Puech made their 'Papou' bag of crocheted raffia with grass skirt fringes, which was very

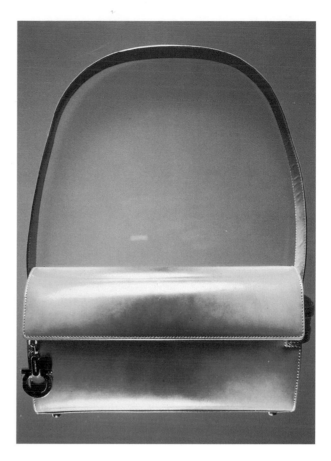

A long, trunk-shape day bag (*above*) with rounded top in bright tangerine by Ferragamo, has a short shoulder strap—the bag sits at the waist—and brass studs at the base.

Black, leather, casual handbag (*left*) by Goldpfeil with double handles, zipped fastening on a curved top and trademark golden arrow.

143

Soft leather, practical, beige day bags with adjustable shoulder straps, matching make-up bag and briefcase-style locks, Jil Sander.

Large and small handbag (*below*) made from the Daks check, plasticized canvas with leather trim, and accompanying silk foulard.

popular with models such as Christy Turlington and Estelle Hallyday, while Bottega Veneta's straw bag with leather trimmings was inspired by a fisherman's creel. Lulu Guinness' shell and starfish decorated, straw bucket bags were too good for the beach, but fine for a stroll along the pier.

By the summer of 1995, the shiny white patent so loved in the 1960s had been revived, seen in Dollargrand's shoppers and Katherine Hamnett's mini bags matched by high, strappy shoes in white patent. Improvements in patents and plastics had made the materials more supple, and Bill Amberg solved the old problem of white bags becoming dirty by coating the leather of his shiny white puffer bags with a wipe clean surface.

The homely beach bag also attracted attention in the mid decade when Pratesi's royal blue beach towel and matching drawstring bag with striped cord became a raging success. Thereafter, bags with co-ordinating towels abounded, from Emilio Pucci's wild print and Ferragamo's leather lattice bag with removable terry cloth insert in four colors to examples from Gianni Versace, Chanel (quilted, of course), Escada, and Guess Home Collection.

Bejeweled Bags for Night

Sequins, crystals, cut stones, and embroideries lit up evening bags of the early 1990s, both in Paris and in Britain. Yves St Laurent Accessoires Couture, Junko Koshino, Paloma Picasso, Nina Ricci, and Renaud Pellegrino were the French favorites, with pink satin and black velvet bags embellished with jewels from Lacroix and Hervé Léger producing embroidered,

Black, hide handbag (*left*) with nickel, metal rod, based on the traditional English music case, but softer and more refined—for the working woman who does not want to look too executive, made in England by Margaret Howell, 1990s.

Small, hand-made conker evening bag (*above*) of silk dupion, lined with duchesse satin—this special bag, for weddings and balls, is one of designer, Emily Jo Gibbs', own favorites, 1993-4.

Simple, 50s inspired, mock croc swing bag (*right*), Katherine Hamnett, 1996.

Black, leather, casual handbag (*above*) by Goldpfeil with double handles, zipped fastening on the curved top and trademark golden arrow—Goldpfeil was the first leather workshop to introduce a brand name article.

crystal and sequinned bags for Daniel Swarowski. Old fashioned, American firms such as Tiffany featured emerald, grosgrain bags.

Evening accessories shone, with drawstring bags in jewel-like colors of emerald, ruby, amber, topaz, and amethyst, while the British costume jewelers, Fior, featured gold- and silver-plated, pavé evening bags. Velvet was a favorite in 1993, found in Armani's velvet pouch, dévoré scarves, dresses, and palazzo pants, as well as silk-lined, ribbed velvet, drawstring pouches with silk cord from Natasha Barrault at Browns.

In Britain, a group of individual, young designers such as Emily Jo Gibbs emerged. Emily Jo Gibbs' bags were almost portable jewels, using silver, copper, and silks in tiny exquisite bags. Part individual craftsman pieces, part commercial accessories, Gibbs' bags sold from New York and Brown's in London.

Multi-functional, Snap Top Fastening Bags

By the mid 1990s, there was a return to 1950s snap-fastening shapes, complete with mirror and Judith Leiber-like diamanté compact. While Judith Leiber's evening bags were instantly recognizable, and took on the status of highly collectible treasures, there were also stylish evening bags from Gianni Versace and Donna Karan, whose wrist bags dangled lightly from the wrist, leaving the hand free to hold drinks, and cigarettes.

In keeping with the vintage look, old-fashioned, grosgrain or brocade bags were remade or borrowed from grandmother, complete with silver frames, snap-top fastening, and chain. Bill Amberg offered up his ribbon lace handbags, there was luxurious printed satin from Lulu Guinness, and Erickson Beamon developed a range of expensive but exquisite bags, such as a gold-plated, solid mesh bag that was like a medieval treasure chest. One new British designer, Matthew Williamson, used antique Parisian beads from the 1920s on his bags.

Envelope-style, simple, flat bags (*above*) in leather with two-tone, fun colors from patrick Cox.

Soft, supple shoulder bags (*above left*) by Jaeger, 1997 in beige and red, laminated leather. Simple, white, laminated leather shopper (*above right)* in open bucket shape, Jaeger, 1997.

A Century of Bags Draws to a Close

From the silver mesh bags of the early years of this century, their ornate metal frames set with exquisite miniature clocks, to the digital clock bag showing the time in Paris and New York (from Marc Gourmelen and Hélène Népomiatzi of 31 Février,) handbags have reflected the changing decades like timekeepers of fashion.

As the century has progressed, they have proved a great unifier, linking shopping mall consumer with supermodel. Not all women can wear high fashion, but bags have never required the perfect figure, and can always update a whole look with minimal expense.

Far from being passé, the structured, ladylike handbag with small, overarm handle was still firmly in place in the late 1990s, its conservative silhouette such that it could have been worn by any generation of 20th century women, albeit without the contemporary bright colors and high sheen. How long it will endure is for time to tell.

Space age, gray leather bag (*below left*) with black nylon interior, Joanna Whitehead. Japanese-inspired design (*center*) in green suede with black leather lettering, Laura Jacometti. Blue/gray and silver bag (*below right*), bead inlaid, by Angela Marti.

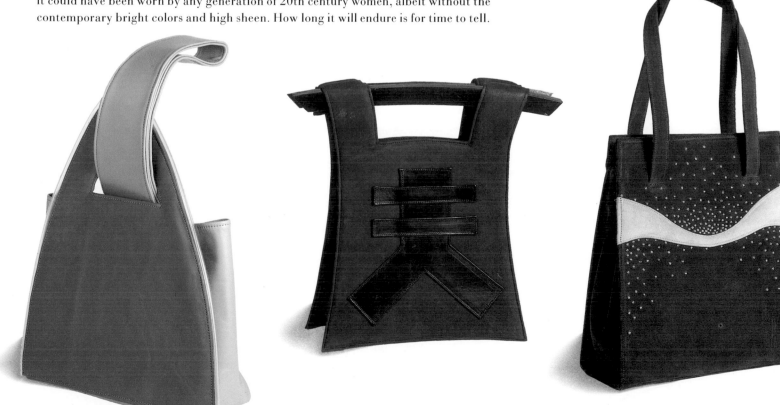

Louis Vuitton canvas rucksack (*below*) with "LV" allover monogram design and leather trimmings, and leather rucksack by The Bridge (*left*)..

Practical Chic with the Backpack

The backpack is practical, sporty, and youthful, as well as presenting a solution to some of life's problems, such as backache and the needs to combine practicality and a fashionable look.

Paul Smith space-age "jug duffel" based on a Bill Amberg design (*above*), and made in bright cotton or ripstop sailcloth.

From the 1980s onwards, the backpack has provided a more subtle fashion statement than the status bags of the early part of the decade. It was also good to wear, with double straps distributing its weight equally between the shoulders. The backpack was made for purposeful striding, as suitable for the serious walker as the serious shopper. By the mid 1980s it was seen everywhere, worn by business women on their way to work, by wandering tourists, and serious walkers, leaving hands free to hold a compass, or a map.

The emergence of the backpack from the unfashionable realms of the hiker was attributed to the Italian designer Miuccia Prada, in 1985. Her revolutionary anti-fashion, black nylon rucksack was at first ignored as it was the antithesis of the sleek, quilted chain bag so popular at the time. It was very modern and downplayed, but was soon spotted on the backs of all those in the know. It could be washed,

it was flexible, it was tough, and it was soft. It seemed to herald in a new age of casual accessories, and by the late 1980s, Prada's fortunes had been turned around by Miuccia Prada's backpack.

Other designers were alert to the possibilities of the backpack, and by 1988, Lancel of Paris had featured their own version. Hervé Chapelier's nylon backpacks were all the rage in 1991, and color began to dominate, moving away from the cool black of the Prada bag. Gucci launched terracotta suede and leather backpacks, and Benetton chunky, brilliantly colored examples in vivid oranges and yellows.

By 1994, when the backpack's popularity had reached its peak, there were examples in crochet, buttery leather, suede, canvas, and patterned cotton on the market. The new softness complemented the fashionable floppy shapes of that summer's clothes. Some were capacious and others tiny—the mini-

A small-scale basketweave variation of the rucksack theme from DKNY (*above*).

A complete back and shoulder collection (*above*) with matching accessories from The Bridge.

rucksack enjoyed a vogue—with just enough room for purse and make-up. Others took the form of cuddly toys, inspired by the doggy versions of designer Anna Sui which had brought a rare smile to the serious face of fashion in the 1980s.

Designer Backpacks

All the top fashion designers produced their own version of the backpack, from baby Gucci —in yellow, pink, and tan leather, with bamboo handle, straps and deep front pocket with toggle fastening—to Emporio Armani's soft, simple, little bags. Donna Karan offered bright white sacks with large, buckled pockets, while Anna Sui designed gold and silver leather mini-rucksacks, and Jamin Puech made fashionable grunge versions in crochet for Ally Cappelino. French designers Hervé Chapelier and Agnes B. made schoolgirl versions, while Esprit's leather rucksacks closed with a top zipper and had an imitation panther pocket. In the later 1990s, the major designers Hermès, Louis Vuitton, Fendi, and Chanel all made distinctively glamorous backpacks. Hermès' "Kelly à dos" knapsack of

1996, for example, was made of black box calfskin and lined in goatskin. More affordable versions were available from chain stores, which made their own in striped canvas and printed cotton. The British store Russell & Bromley was one, famed for decades for their stylish bags, as were the younger chains of Next, Pepe, and Soco. Mini-backpacks were perfect for clubbing, being lightweight and unobtrusive, and became the latest in clubland wear, sold from ultra-fashionable outlets such as the designer thrift shop American Retro in London's Soho, and Stussy's Sista.

It was the egalitarian nature of the backpack that ensured its success. It was a bag that everyone felt comfortable with, that suited every occasion, and that everyone could afford, ranging in price from $15 to $500. Such a breakthrough in the history of fashionable accessories was comparable only to the arrival of denim jeans, which had also started out as functional, practical items of workwear.

Leiber novelty minaudières, like the cat (*right*), in gem-encrusted metal, are now collectors' items.

Gold kid " hatbox" with rhinestone trimmings, 1967 (*below*).

Judith Leiber

Novelty meets charm and elegance in Judith Leiber's creations, many of which have become collectors' items.

Leiber adds a delightfully novel touch to a classic black satin evening bags, with her rhinestone-studded peacock ornaments (*above*).

Judith Leiber was born in Budapest in 1921 and trained as an apprentice at the Hungarian Handbag Guild from 1939 onwards. By the end of her apprenticeship she had become both a journeyman and the first ever woman *Meister* that the Guild recognized. After emigrating to New York in 1947, she designed bags for well-known companies such as Nettie Rosenstein, Richard Kort, and the Morris Moskowitz brothers before launching her own business in 1963.

She went on to win numerous awards for her bags, including the Handbag Designer of the Year Award, 1992, and the Council of Fashion Designers of America Lifetime Achievement Award, 1994. She described herself as someone who loves to design beautiful objects, and her bags have attracted great attention because of the way they combine artistry and art.

Leiber is perhaps best known for her jeweled minaudières for evening wear. The minaudière, from the French word meaning to charm, is a compartmentalized, handheld, metal case, which is believed to have been introduced by Charles Arpels, of the jewelry house of Van Cleef & Arpels, in 1933. The idea for the tiny vanity cases came when he saw the socialite Florence Gould, wife of American railroad magnate Frank J. Gould, throwing her lipstick, powder, and lighter into a large metal box of Lucky Strike cigarettes. The minaudières are evening bags that merge into jewelry, and Leiber herself has worn one of her creations as a necklace. Their interiors are tiny, barely holding more than the matching tasseled comb and gold-edged mirror, lipstick, and $100 dollar bill. As Leiber said, that is all a woman needs.

The creation of the minaudieres is painstaking and costly. Each bag is sculpted in wax, cast in metal, and then goldplated and lined with English kidskin. An intricate design is painted onto the plate before being covered

Suitcase bag, 1990, in orange and chalk embroidered over orange capeskin (*left*).

with 7000-13000 rhinestones, or imitation gems, made by the renowned crystal company of Swarovski, in the Tyrol region of Austria. Each stone is glued on by hand in a process that takes from two to five days.

The glittering, alluring result is an evening bag that requires no identifying logo. Fans of Judith

Japanes *obi* pouch (*above*) which has been re-embroidered with rhinestones, 1990.

Leiber's work recognize these bags from afar, collecting and displaying her minaudières like precious jewels. Museum collections, such as those at the Museum of the City of New York and the Museum at the Fashion Institute of Technology, are equally keen to acquire them.

Variety of Shape
In the 1980s, the new feeling for luxury that emanated from the top costume designers was perfectly complemented by Leiber's evening bags. There are sophisticated classics, such as a satin and rhinestone evening bag of 1994, with bracelet handle, and idiosyncratic marvels, influenced by sources as diverse as fruit and vegetables, nursery rhymes, netsuke purse toggles, the Manhattan skyline, and old Teddy bears. Much of Leiber's work has an element of whimsy, as seen in her egg-shaped "Humpty " bag.
A Bill Blass, sequinned and beaded bolero of 1985 in black and white, was set off to perfection by Leiber's jeweled minaudière in an Art Deco inspired, black and white sunburst pattern. Judith Leiber also makes

sophisticated day bags, taking a great sensual delight in their materials. Her bags celebrate the luxurious qualities of reptile and ostrich skins, calfskin, goat and suede, fantastic embroidery, pleating, braiding, and trims, sometimes finishing them with humorous, dangling charms, such as telephones and typewriters for business women. Each bag can contain up to 100 components, and each one is handcut, interlined, handstitched, lined, and finally polished into styles as various as large, polished alligator totes and bucket bags, "lunch boxes" and "umbrella" cases. Most have discreetly hidden shoulder straps as well as handles.

Her price range is huge—anywhere from hundreds to thousands of dollars —but the small company is still based in the shabby handbag district of New York, off Fifth Avenue, Manhattan. From there, she provides her gleaming leather handbags and kooky, encrusted evening bags for a limited few, although once seen in public, for the pleasure of many.

Typical of Prada's minimalist style (*left*), from the Fall/Winter 1997-1998

High-luster satin shoulder bags (*right*), 1997 Collection.

Prada

Prada tradition lies in the finest quality, but its survival in the modern world owes much to a simple, anti-fashion, nylon backpack.

Rich fabric overarm bags with vertical pattern (*above*).

In 1913, Mario Prada established the leatherwork company of Fratelli Prada in Milan, Italy. He was determined to use only the finest materials to make his exclusive pieces of baggage, and traveled the world over seeking out the finest skins that money could buy.

By the 1920s and 1930s, the European aristocracy and royalty regularly patronized his upmarket Milan store, buying the Prada suitcases and steamer trunks that were the epitome of luxury travel goods. They were so heavy they relied on armies of servants to carry them and unpack their precious contents, kitted out with tortoiseshell, ivory, and gold fittings. By the 1950s, however, a diminishing demand for such leatherwork after two world wars left Fratelli Prada manufacturing bags and accessories in styles of greatly diminished grandeur, but still of the highest quality.

When Miuccia Prada took over the family business in 1978, the prognosis for the company did not look good. Business had been gradually dwindling, and Miuccia seemed an unlikely candidate to revitalize Prada. She had been highly educated by her wealthy family—her doctorate from Milan University was in political science—and was both a feminist and a member of the Communist party in the 1970s. She had no intention of becoming a fashion designer, or working for the family. "Making bags or shoes or dresses was the worst way I could spend my time," she is quoted as saying. "I was embarrassed, since most fashion had been such a nightmare for women. And I never actually decided to become a designer. Eventually I found out that I was one."

Miuccia's breakthrough design, in the mid 1980s, was for a nylon backpack, the antithesis of all that Prada had stood for. At first ignored, it began gradually to take on the status of a cult bag. Black, lightweight, practical, unlined, and at first with no identifying logo or monogram, it was made by machine in a parachute factory at a time when conspicuous consumption was endemic in the accessory world. As the bag's identity began to grow, a flat metal tag, taken from the early trunks that her grandfather had made, was added, and an icon was born.

Inspired by Chanel, Miucca designed a range of quilted, industrial nylon bags with chain straps fed through reinforced giant eyelets. They were modern and very Italian, in bright orange, red, and yellow. Inside each bag was a small, leather-bound book outlining the history of the company. .

Adored by fashion enthusiasts and widely copied, Prada bags also inspired a fetishistic delight. Her cult shopper of the 1990s, featured famously in Peter Lindberg's

advertisement of 1991 for Prada, was described as "both a cult item and subliminally sexual: all black nylon and little zippers." Prada imitations were rife, and the company sought to stamp out counterfeiting by telling shoppers to beware. The genuine article, they said, could be identified by a white authenticity card with code number, heavy chains threaded with leather, a solid Prada label on the front of the bag, and a drawstring Prada dust cover.

In the late 1980s, Prada branched out with great success into producing their first clothes collections, the clothes reflecting the same considered, understated tone as the bags. They went on to set up a series of stores, called Miu Miu after Miuccia's nickname, through which they sold the diffusion range in the mid 1990s, featuring large, glossy shoulder bags with large buckles.

Plastic chain bags followed, then patent leather mini-shoppers and bucket bags in 1995. During a vogue for transparency, Prada launched the reveal-all holdall, a perfectly simple square with top handles stamped with "Prada, Milano" and very little else. For a time, it was the most desirable plastic bag in the world, complete with opaque cream nylon purse with curved frame and snap fastening.

It is not clear why Prada's bags inspired such desire and delight. Perhaps it was because of their simplicity and purity in a decade of excess, or because of the hype of the fashion world. More likely, it was because Miuccia Prada, steeped in the heady combination of a family history of accessory making and her own political feminism, understood what women really wanted.

Printed satin, day-into-evening bags with oriental-style leaf motifs and delicate, metal twist-knob fastenings and handles (below).

Classic, green sam, black vertical shopper and brown heather large sam (*above*), merino wool jersey knit with bengaline lining.

Kate Spade

American designer, Kate Spade, is one of New York's hottest handbag properties. In 1996, she won the Perry Ellis Award for New Fashion Talent in accessories, placing her at the forefront of the American fashion scene.

Sturdy, two-tone, medium bucket (*above*), made of heavy weight 100% cotton.

Her fashionable bag range is inspired by a combination of an early love of vintage bags and a desire to create practical, stylish bags that do not cost the earth.

Kate Brosnahan began her professional life as a fashion journalist. After gaining a journalism degree in Kansas City, she moved to Manhattan to work for the fashion magazine Mademoiselle for five years. By the early 1990s, as Senior Fashion Editor and Head of Accessories, she had noticed a gap in the handbag market. Instinct and research told her that there was a demand for classically-shaped handbags in unexpected colors and fabrics. She left journalism, and in January 1993, created her own line of handbags. "My goal was to create bags that I could never find when I worked as an editor," she explains.

She formed a professional partnership with her then boyfriend, Andy Spade, an advertising man who had been dubbed by the magazine *Adweek*, as "the best copywriter in America." He became President and Creative Director of the newly formed Kate Spade company, and shortly afterwards he and Kate married. As a husband-and-wife team, they say, "We are able to combine my marketing background with Kate's design sensibility to create smart handbags with a timeless yet unique appeal."

More specifically, for Kate, she sees her products as lying between the casual "preppie" style of LL Bean and the elegance of Prada in both design and price, without resembling eachother. Her determination to keep prices down and her lateral thinking on materials has resulted in some wonderfully creative variations on a classical theme of alternative materials to leather. She maximizes the potential of the fabrics in season—from thick wool melton, Liberty prints, and Harris tweeds to oilskin, linen, and nylon—by incorporating them into her designs.

The first Kate Spade creations to hit the fashion scene were nylon tote bags which were an immediate success, minimally designed, functional, affordable, and in neutral colors, grass greens and bright oranges. She was soon discovered by store buyers, and her range expanded to include satin evening bags with a snap top fastening and chain handle, linen and nylon shoulder bags, backpacks, novasuede shoppers, and canvas totes.

Young, fashionable, and individualistic, Kate Spade has brought her personal vision of handbags to life, much like her London contemporaries Lulu Guinness, Bill Amberg, and Anya Hindmarch. In contrast to the mass-produced bags of the late 1990s, Spade's bags are clearly created by someone whose Mid West influence has injected an inspirational, fresh approach to design, yet the bags remain classic enough to be accessible to the streets of Manhattan. The company is now poised to tap the global market—in 1997 they launched in Japan and Soho, New York. "The challenge," explains Andy, "is to grow the brand without disrupting its unique image. It's really about creating a personality that extends beyond a handbag."

Small, classic, orange shopper (*below*), 100% authentic Harris Tweed Wool.

Brown/camel dutchess (*below left*), made of 100% Irish Houndstooth Wool.

Burgundy, gingham-lined Claire (*below right*), made of traditional cotton seeksucker.

Index

Credits

Key: a above, b below, r right, l left, c centre m middle

Adidas 110bl, 111r The Advertising Archives 8a, 121ar
Angela Marti 147br Asprey 49al Bill Amberg 126bl,
126ac, 126ar, 127br, 127ar The Bridge 65ar, 136al,
137ar, 148al, 149ar Bruno Magli 116al, 116bl, 139ar,
139br, 142br Cartier 105ar Chanel 14bl, 66al, 66ar,
66bl, 67 Charles Jourdan 123br, 125al Corbis UK Ltd 16,
21bl, 26, 31ar, 40, 44, 47ar, 54, 60bl, 68, 73al, 94al,
81, 86, 88, 100, 114, 132, DAKS Simpson Ltd 11br,
141al, 145br DKNY 1, 65br, 134al, 149al Dooney and
Bourke 64bl, 125al Emily Jo Gibbs 142a, 146al Esprit
138br Etienne Aigner 116br Fendi 122al Ferragamo 139l,
139br, 143a Ghurka 64, 123ar, 124bl, 124ar Goldpfeil
14al, 96ar, 97, 140bl, 141br, 143b, 146bl Gucci 130bl,
130ar, 131al, 131br Hermès, Paris 98bl, 98ar, 99bl,
99br Image Select 32bl Jacobson 102ar Jaeger 147al
Jane Shilton 108a, 120bl, 135al, 135ar Jill Sander
118b, 145al, 145ar Joan & David 10, 117ar, 119al,
122bl Joanna Whitehead 147bl Judith Leiber 13, 14ar,
50bl, 117br, 150bl, 150ac, 150acr, 151a, 151b
Karimoor 110ar Katherine Hamnett 146ar S. Launer & Co.
82l, 82r, 83a, 83b Laura Jacometti 147Longchamp 11cr,
134br, 137al, 141ar Louis Vuitton 120ar, 125bl, 128cr,
128ar, 128b, 129al, 129acl, 129acr, 129bcl, 129bc,
129bcr, 148ar Lulu Guinness 84al, 84ar, 84b, 85a, 85b
Margaret Howell 144 Mary Quant 88bl Moschino 121al,
123al, 136ar, 138al Mulberry 113ar,113bl Patrick Cox
64al, 96bl, 138bl, 140ar, 147ar Paul Smith/Aboud-
Sodano 15a, 111l, 140, 142bl, 148bl Prada 15b, 152al,
152ar, 152bl, 153 Sears Roebuck 23bl Tassenmuseum
Hendrikje, Holland/Sigrid Ivo 8b, 9al, 9ar, 11a, 12al,
20ar, 20bl, 21al, 21br, 23ar, 25br, 30, 31br, 34ar, 39,
43br, 47c, 51, 76br, 92al, 95bl William Doyle Galleries,
New York 53

We would like to thank and acknowledge the following
handbag collectors and suppliers who very kindly lent us
bags for photography;

Beauty and the Beasts18bl, 28, 29, 30bl, 33ar, 33br,
35br, 37, 49br, 59br, 52ar, 76ar, 76b, 78cr, 91bl Moira
Clinch 36bl, 70bl Cornucopia 20b, 28bl, 42bl, 43ar,
44al, 46al, 46bl, 50ar, 56al, 57ar, 71ar, 73ac, 73br,
74bl, 75, 77, 78bl, 79cl, 90al, 80bl, 80ar, 103br, 106al,
121br Fior 60al, 61br, 91br, 94cl, 94cr, 94b, 102bl,

104br, 106bl, 107a, 107b, 108b, 118al, 119ar Annie
Hawker 112 Linda Bee 6, 9br, 22l, 22r, 24al, 24ar, 31al,
32al, 34br, 43bl, 45ar, 47b, 48bl, 57br, 58al, 59ar,
59bl, 60br, 61al, 62al, 62br, 62bl, 69, 70al, 71al, 72al,
72bl, 73, 76bl, 77al, 78al, 78ac, 78ar, 78cl,78mc,
78bc, 78br, 91ar, 92br, 93ar, 101, 109b, 115, 119br,
133 Steinberg & Tolkein 2, 17, 19b, 24bl, 25al, 27,
30br, 35al, 41, 45br, 48br, 52, 55, 56bl, 63al, 63br,
74a, 74al, 77br, 79br, 90bc, 92bl, 93al, 95ar, 95br, 87,
103al, 104ar, 104bl, 105br, 109a

The handbag suppliers can be reached at the following
addresses:

Beauty and the Beasts
Stalls Q9-Q10, Antiquarius Antique Centre
141 Kings Road, London SW3

Cornucopia
12 Upper Tachbrook Street, London SW1V

Fior
27 Brompton Road, London SW3

Linda Bee
Grays Mews Antiques Market,
1-7 Davies Mews, London W1

Steinberg & Tolkein
193 Kings Road, London SW3

We would especially like to thank Linda Bee for her
valuable help and expertise, Fior and Steinberg & Tolkein
for their advice, and Marley and Linda Hodgson of Ghurka
for their enthusiasm with this project.

Lastly we would like to acknowledge the Tassenmuseum
Hendrikje, Amstelveen, Holland, for their invaluable
contribution to this book. The museum houses over a
thousand bags and purses, showing developments in
design from the middle ages to the present day. The
collection includes work by designers including Chanel,
Whiting & Davis, Elsa Schiaparelli, Pierre Cardin, Paco
Rabanne, as well as rare animal skin, straw, shell,
beaded, papier-mâché, ivory and plastic bags.